ALSO BY PATTI SMITH

The New Jerusalem

Devotion

M Train

Just Kids

Auguries of Innocence

Collected Lyrics, 1970–2015

The Coral Sea

Early Work

Woolgathering

Babel

Wītt

Seventh Heaven

Kodak

Year of the Monkey

Year of the Monkey

PATTI SMITH

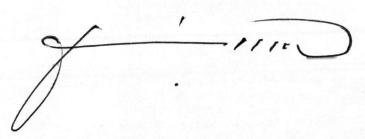

VINTAGE BOOKS
A Division of Penguin Random House LLC
New York

FIRST VINTAGE BOOKS EDITION, SEPTEMBER 2020

The Library of Congress has cataloged
the Knopf edition as follows:
Names: Smith, Patti, author.
Title: Year of the monkey / Patti Smith.
Description: First edition. | New York: Alfred A. Knopf, 2019.
Identifiers: LCCN 2019009856 (print) | LCCN 2019018498 (ebook)
Subjects: LCSH: Smith, Patti. | Poets, American—20th century—
Biography. | Women rock musicians—United States—Biography.
Classification: LCC PS3569.M53787 (ebook) | LCC PS3569.M53787 Z46
2019 (print) | DDC 818/.5403 B—dc23
LC record available at https://lccn.loc.gov/2019009856

Vintage Books Trade Paperback ISBN: 978-1-9848-9892-0
eBook ISBN: 978-0-525-65769-9

Book design by Cassandra J. Pappas

www.vintagebooks.com

Printed in the United States of America
10   9   8   7   6   5   4   3   2   1

A mortal folly comes over the world.

—ANTONIN ARTAUD

Contents

Year of the Monkey

WAY OUT WEST

It was well past midnight when we pulled up in front of the Dream Motel. I paid the driver, made sure I left nothing behind, and rang the bell to wake up the proprietor. It's almost 3 a.m., she said, but gave me my key and a bottle of mineral water. My room was on the lowest floor, facing the long pier. I opened the sliding glass door and could hear the sound of the waves accompanied by the faint barking of sea lions sprawled out on the planks beneath the wharf. Happy New Year! I called out. Happy New Year to the waxing moon, the telepathic sea.

The drive from San Francisco was just over an hour. I had been wide awake but suddenly felt beat. I took off my coat and left the sliding door slightly open to listen to the waves but immediately fell into a facsimile of sleep. I awoke abruptly, went to the john, brushed my teeth, removed my boots and went to bed. Maybe I dreamed.

New Year's morning in Santa Cruz, pretty dead. I had a sudden desire for a particular breakfast: black coffee, grits with green onions. Not much chance for such fare here but a plate of ham and eggs would do. I grabbed my camera and walked down the hill toward the pier. A sign partially obscured by tall, slim palms loomed, and I realized this was not a motel after all. The sign said *Dream Inn*, punctuated by a starburst reminiscent of the *Sputnik* era. I stopped to admire it and took a Polaroid, unpeeled the image and slipped it in my pocket.

—Thank you, Dream Motel, I said, half to the air, half to the sign.

—It's the Dream Inn! the sign exclaimed.

— Oh yeah, sorry, I said, somewhat taken aback. Even so, I didn't dream a thing.

—Oh really? Nothing!

—Nothing!

I could not help feeling like Alice interrogated by the hookah-smoking caterpillar. I looked down at my feet, avoiding the sign's scrutinizing energy.

—Well, thanks for the picture, I said, preparing to shove off.

However, my departure was derailed by a sudden popping-up of animated Tenniel: The upright Mock Turtle. The fish and frog servants. The Dodo decked in his one grand jacket sleeve, the horrid Duchess and the Cook, and

Alice herself, glumly presiding over an endless tea party, where, pardon us all, no tea was being served. I wondered if the sudden bombardment was self-induced or courtesy of the magnetic charge of the Dream Inn sign.

— And what about now?

—The mind! I cried out, exasperated as the animated sketches multiplied at an alarming rate.

— The waking mind! the sign chortled triumphantly.

I turned away, breaking the transmission. In truth, being somewhat wall-eyed, I often witness such leaping about, most often to the right. Besides, once fully roused, the brain is receptive to all kinds of signals, but I wasn't about to confess that to a sign.

—I didn't dream anything! I shouted back stubbornly, heading down the hill flanked by floating salamanders.

At the bottom of the hill was a low-slung joint with the word *coffee* horizontally spelled out in letters over a foot high across the glass, with a sign beneath that said Open. Having devoted so much window space to the word *coffee*, I reasoned they might serve a pretty good cup and maybe even donuts dusted in cinnamon. But as I put my hand on the doorknob, I noticed a smaller sign dangling: Closed. No explanation, no *back in twenty minutes*. I had a bad feeling about prospects for coffee, and zero for donuts. I supposed most people were tucked away with a hangover. One can't begrudge a café for being closed on New Year's Day, although it seemed that coffee would be the exact remedy needed after a night of excessive reveling.

Coffee denied, I sat on the outside bench going over the edges of the night before. It was the last of three nights in a row performing at the Fillmore and I was pulling the strings off my Stratocaster when some guy with a greasy ponytail leaned over and puked on my boots. The last gasp of 2015, a spray of vomit ushering in the New Year. A good or bad sign? Well, considering the state of the world, who could tell the difference? Reminded of this, I rummaged through my pockets for a witch-hazel wipe, usually reserved for cleaning my camera lens, knelt down and cleaned up my boots. Happy New Year, I told them.

Softly treading past the sign, a curious chain of phrases came zipping in and I dug into my pockets for a pencil, thinking to get them down. *Ashen birds circling the city dusted with night / Vagrant meadows adorned with mist / A mythic palace that was yet a forest / Leaves that are but leaves.* It's the dried-up-poet syndrome, necessitating plucking inspiration from the erratic air, like Jean Marais in Cocteau's *Orpheus,* shutting himself up in a baroque garage on the outskirts of Paris in a battered Rolls-Royce, tuning in to the radio's frequencies and scribbling fragments on slips of paper—*a drop of water contains the world, etc.*

Back in my room I located some tubes of Nescafé and a small electric pot. I made my own coffee, wrapped myself in a blanket, opened the sliding doors and sat on the little patio facing the sea. There was a low wall partially obstructing the view, but I had my coffee, could hear the waves and was reasonably content.

Then I thought of Sandy. He was supposed to be here, in a room down the hall. We were going to meet in San Francisco before the band's run at the Fillmore and do our usual things: have coffee at Caffè Trieste, peruse the shelves of the City Lights Bookstore and drive back and forth across the Golden Gate listening to the Doors and Wagner and the Grateful Dead. Sandy Pearlman, the fellow I had known for over four decades, with his speedy cadence breaking down the *Ring* cycle or a Benjamin Britten riff, was always there when we played the Fillmore, in his slouchy leather jacket and baseball cap, hunched over a glass of ginger ale at his usual table behind a curtain near the dressing room. We had intended to break rank after the New Year's Eve concert and drive late that night through the seething mist to Santa Cruz. The plan was to have New Year's Day lunch at his secret taco place not far from the Dream Motel.

But that never happened, for Sandy had been found alone, on the eve of our first concert, unconscious in a parking lot in San Rafael. He was taken to a hospital in Marin County, having suffered a cerebral hemorrhage.

The morning of our first concert Lenny Kaye and I went to the ICU in Marin County. Sandy in a coma with tubes everywhere, enveloped in eerie silence. We stood on either side of him, promising to mentally hold on to him, keep an open channel, ready to intercept and accept any signal. Not just shards of love, as Sandy would say, but the whole goblet.

We drove back to our hotel in Japantown, hardly able to speak. Lenny picked up his guitar and we headed to a place called On the Bridge located on the walkway connecting the east and west mall. We sat in the back at a green wooden table, both of us in quiet shock. The walls were yellow, hung with posters from Japanese manga, *Hell Girl* and *Wolf's Rain* and rows of comics that were more like paperback novels. Lenny had katsu curry with Asahi Super Dry beer and I had flying-fish-roe spaghetti and oolong tea. We ate, solemnly shared a sake, then walked over to the Fillmore for our sound check. There was nothing we could do but pray and play without Sandy's enthusing presence. We plunged into the first of three nights of feedback, poetry, improvisational rants, politics, and rock 'n' roll, with a relentlessness that left me breathless, as if we could sonically reach him.

On the morning of my sixty-ninth birthday, Lenny and I went back to the hospital. We stood by Sandy's bed and, despite the impossibility, vowed not to leave him. Lenny and I found each other's eyes, knowing we couldn't really stay. There was work to be done, concerts to perform, lives to live, however carelessly. We were condemned to celebrate my sixty-ninth birthday at the Fillmore without him. That night, momentarily turning my back on the crowd during the breakdown of *If 6 Was 9,* I held back tears as streams of words superimposed over other streams, overlapping with images of Sandy, still unconscious, just a Golden Gate away.

When we finished our work in San Francisco, I left Sandy behind and headed to Santa Cruz on my own. I couldn't bring myself to cancel his room, and I sat in the back of the car with his voice swirling. *Matrix Monolith Medusa Macbeth Metallica Machiavelli.* Sandy's own M game, straight to the velvet tassel, with instructions taking him all the way to the Library of Imaginos.

I sat on my patio, wrapped in a blanket like a convalescent in *The Magic Mountain,* then felt the genesis of a strange headache, most likely a sudden change in the barometer. I headed to the front desk in pursuit of an aspirin when I noticed that my room was not on the ground floor but on the subfloor beneath, making it closer to the edge where the beach began. I had forgotten this and became confused while walking the length of the dimly lit hall. Unable to locate the stairwell leading to the reception desk, I gave up on the aspirin and decided to go back. Going for my key, I found a tight roll of gauze about as thick as a Gauloises. I unwound a third of it, half expecting to find a message, but there was nothing. I had no idea how it came to be in my pocket, but rewound it, slipped it back and reentered my room. I turned on the radio and Nina Simone was singing *I Put a Spell on You*. The seals were silent, and I could hear the waves in the distance, winter on the West Coast. I sank into bed and slept heavily.

In the Dream Motel, I was certain I did not dream, yet the more I thought about it, I realized I did dream. More precisely, I skated along the fringe of dream. Dusk masqueraded as night, unmasking as dawn and illuming a path I willingly followed, from the desert to the sea. Gulls were wailing and cawing as the seals slept, save their king, more like a walrus, who lifted his head and bellowed at the sun. There was a sense of everyone gone, a J. G. Ballard kind of gone.

The beach was littered with candy wrappers, hundreds of them, maybe thousands, scattering the beach like feathers after a molt. I crouched down to investigate, pocketing a handful. Butterfingers, Peanut Chews, 3 Musketeers, Milky Ways and Baby Ruths. All opened yet not a trace of chocolate. There was no one around, no footprints on the shore, only a boom box partially obscured by a mound of sand. I had forgotten my key, but the sliding door was unlocked. When I reentered my room, I could see that I was still sleeping, so I waited, with the window open, till I awoke.

My dual-self continued to dream, even under my own watchful eye. I came upon a fading billboard announcing that the candy-wrapper phenomenon had spread all the way to San Diego, covering a small stretch of beach I knew well, adjacent to the OB fishing pier. I followed a footpath through unending marshes dotted with abandoned high-rises with shifting angles. Long, slender weed trees grew from cracks in the cement, branches like pale arms protruding from dead structures. By the time I got to the beach the moon had risen, silhouetting the old pier. I was too late, all evidence of the wrappers had been raked into mounds and set aflame, creating a long line of toxic bonfires that nonetheless looked quite beautiful, the ignited wrappers curling like artificial autumn leaves.

The fringe of dream, an evolving fringe at that! Maybe more of a visitation, a prescience of things to come, like a tremendous swarm of gnats, black clouds obscuring the paths of children reeling on bicycles. The borders of reality had reconfigured in such a way that it seemed necessary to map out the patchwork topography. What was needed was a bit of geometric thinking to lay it all out. In the back of the desk drawer were a couple of Band-Aids, a faded postcard, a stick of carbon, and a folded sheet of tracing paper, which seemed like unbelievable luck. I taped the tracing paper to the wall, attempting to make sense of an impossible scape, but composed nothing more than a fractured diagram containing all the improbable logic of a child's treasure map.

—Use your head, chided the mirror.

—Use your mind, counseled the sign.

A J. G. Ballard kind of gone

My pocket was stuffed with candy wrappers. I spread them out on the desk next to the postcard, the San Diego Panama Exposition of 1915, which set me to thinking that maybe I should go to San Diego and check out Ocean Beach myself.

In the course of my fruitless analytics I had worked up quite an appetite. I found a retro diner nearby called Lucy's and settled on a grilled cheese on rye, blueberry pie and black coffee. In the booth behind me were some kids, maybe in their early teens. I hadn't paid attention to what they were saying, more lulled by the sound of their voices, as if drifting from the jukebox, a coin-operated song selector, mounted to the table. The jukebox kids were talking low, a hum that gradually manifested as words.

—No, it's two words, an adjective-noun combination.

—No way, they are two different words, it's not a combination, it's just two different things. One's an adjective and one's a noun.

—That's the same thing.

—No, you said combo. It's not a combo. They're separate.

—You're all boneheads, said a new voice. Sudden silence. He must have had clout, because they all shut up and listened.

—It's a thing. A description. It's a thing, I'm telling you. Candy wrapper is a noun.

That got my attention. Happenstance or what? The hum

rose like vapors from a block of dry ice. I picked up my check and casually stopped at their booth. Four aggressively cool nerds.

—Hey know anything about this? I said, smoothing out a wrapper.

—They spelled Chews wrong. With a Z.

—You know where it might have come from?

—Maybe some Chinese knockoff.

—Well, if you hear anything let me know.

As they eyed me with mounting amusement I picked up the phony Peanut Chews wrapper. Somehow, I hadn't spotted the errant Z. The woman at the register was opening a roll of quarters. I realized I had forgotten to leave a tip and returned to my booth.

—By the way, I said, stopping in front of them, candy wrapper is definitely a noun.

They got up and brushed past me leaving no tip. I noticed they each had a blue backpack with a vertical yellow stripe. The last one to leave glared at me. He had dark wavy hair, his right eye slightly wandering, somewhat like my own.

My phone was vibrating. It was Lenny calling with a report on Sandy, which was no report at all. Stable silence requiring patience and prayer. I wandered into a thrift store, impulsively buying an old Grateful Dead tie-dye T-shirt with Jerry Garcia's face on it. There were two small bookcases in the back with stacks of *National Geographic*,

Stephen King books, video games and random CDs. I found a couple of back issues of *Biblical Archaeology Review* and a worn paperback of Gérard de Nerval's *Aurélia*. Everything was cheap except the Jerry t-shirt, but it was worth the price, his smiling face reeking of chemical love.

Back in my room I was surprised that someone had untaped my diagram from the wall and rolled it up. I laid the Jerry shirt on my pillow, plopped in the easy chair and opened *Aurélia*, but barely got past the alluring first sentence. *Our dreams are a second life.* I dozed off briefly into a revolution dream, the French one that is, with young fellows dressed in flowing shirts and leather breeches. Their leader is bound to a heavy gate with leather straps. A follower approaches him with a torch, holding it steady as the flame burns through the thick binding. The leader is freed, his wrists black and bubbling. He calls out to his horse, then tells me he has formed a band called Glitter Noun.

—Why Glitter? I say. Sparkle is better.

—Yeah but Sparklehorse already used up Sparkle.

—Why not just plain Noun?

—Noun. I like it, says the leader. Noun it is.

He mounts his spotted Appaloosa, wincing as the reins fall across his wrist.

—Take care of that, I say.

He has dark wavy hair and one wandering eye. He nods and rides off with his band toward the distant pampas, stopping to draw water from a rough stream where the same misspelled wrappers turn in the current like small multi-colored fish.

I woke abruptly and checked the time, hardly a dent. Distractedly I picked up one of the Bible archaeology magazines. I've always enjoyed reading them, like offshoots of detective digests, always on the verge of uncovering an Aramaic fragment or tracking down the remains of Noah's Ark. The cover was pretty enticing. *Death at the Dead Sea! Was King Saul impaled on the wall of Beth Shean?* Searching my memory, I could hear the resounding mantra of the women, celebrating as their men returned from battle. *Saul has slain his thousands, and David his tens of thousands.* I checked the drawer for a Gideon Bible but it was in Spanish, when I remembered that Saul, having been wounded by an enemy arrow, purposely fell upon his sword, saving himself the humiliation of being mocked and tortured by the Philistines.

I scanned my room searching for another diversion, then grabbed my blanket and returned to the patio, spending several minutes examining the Peanut Chewz wrapper but channeling nothing. I had the distinct feeling that something was going to happen. I feared it would be a piercing event, a right-out-of-the-blue thing or worse, a profound nonevent. I shuddered thinking of Sandy.

Hours slipped by. I went for a walk, half circling the hotel and passing the plaque honoring Jack O'Neill, the famous surfer who invented a new kind of wetsuit. I tried to

Ayers Rock, Uluru

picture surfers from old *Gidget* movies. Did Troy Donahue wear a wetsuit? Did Moondoggie? Did they actually surf? I was careful to avoid glancing up at the Dream Motel sign, when the wind suddenly picked up, the palms bent and swayed and I was assaulted by a temperate haughtiness.

—Dreaming in, are we?

—No, not a thing, I insisted. No dreams. No dreams. All is the same as it was, nothing has happened at all.

The sign became absolutely animated, prodding me with insinuations, leading questions, riddling my mind with obsolete phone numbers and demanding to know the sequencing of certain albums, such as the song before *White Rabbit*, or the song between *Queen Jane Approximately* and *Just Like Tom Thumb's Blues*. What was it actually? Oh, *Ballad of a Thin Man*. No, that wasn't right at all, but the thought of it brought the chorus looping—*something is happening, but you don't know what it is*. Most likely just another piece of provocation. Somehow that darn sign was aware of everything, my comings and goings, the contents of my pockets, including the wrappers, my 1922 silver dollar and a fragment of the red skin of Ayers Rock, that I had not yet found, on a walking path in Uluru, where I had not yet walked.

—When are you leaving? It's a very long flight, you know.

—Wherever do you mean? I'm not going anywhere, I said smugly, attempting to conceal any thoughts of future travel, but the great monolith stubbornly crowned, surfacing in my mental sea like a drunken submarine.

—You're going! I see it! The writing is on the wall. Red dust everywhere. One need only read the signs.

—How can you possibly know that? I demanded, completely exasperated.

—Uncommon sense, replied the sign. And please! Uluru! It's the dream capital of the world. Naturally you're going!

An amorous couple passed by, and just like that the sign was simply a sign, mute and unassailable. I stood before it assessing the situation. The trouble with dreaming, I was thinking, is that one can be drawn into a mystery that is no mystery at all, occasioning absurd observations and discourse leading to not a single reality-based conclusion. It was all too reminiscent of the labyrinthine banter of Alice and the Mad Hatter.

On the other hand, the sign had gleaned my all-too-real desire to journey to the center of the Australian wilderness to see Ayers Rock. Sam Shepard often spoke of his solitary trek to Uluru, and how one day we might go together, lingering in border towns, driving through the outback and skirting the edges of the spinifex-starred plains. But Sam had been stricken with ALS, and as his physical challenges mounted, all loosely woven plans unraveled. I wondered if destiny, in the voice of the sign, was suggesting the possibility that I might yet see the great red monolith on my own, surely taking Sam along, secured in some uncharted sector of my being.

IT WAS TIME to find something to eat. I bypassed the active pier and walked aimlessly down some side streets, stopping before the Las Palmas Taco Bar. Somehow, though I had never been there, the place seemed familiar. I sat in the back and ordered black beans and fish tacos. The coffee had an Aztec chocolate edge. Definitely a Sandy thing. Could this be his secret taco place? Something seemed to have a hand in my so-called improvised movements. I had a second cup, drinking it slowly, beginning to feel irrationally attached to the Dream Motel perimeter. I better get out of here, I was thinking, lest I wind up like the soldier in *The Magic Mountain* who goes up a hill and never comes down. I closed my eyes, picturing my room, and could see the sliding door opening onto the roar of the waves obscured by a low wall, just a cement wall, maybe whitewashed, unless cement can be white in itself.

—It can be any color, for goodness' sake. Pigments. Pigments.

Had that damn sign followed me all the way to Front Street?

—Did you say pigmeats? I whispered. A strange by-the-sea gastronomic suggestion. You should be talking a blue-plate special with mackerel and some of that darn obligatory coleslaw, a dish I've never relished.

—Coleslaw is not a dish, it's a side. And it's PIGMENT, not pigmeat.

Refusing any further transmission, I gulped my coffee, paid my check and hurried back. I had a few words for that sign in person.

—You seem a bit nettled, I said, gaining the upper hand. The sign sniffed.

—And looking pallid as well. You could use a little pigment yourself, perhaps a dab of cerulean blue to touch up your sorry star.

—Humph. I could tell you a thing or two about pigments, piped the sign. For instance, the secret color of water, and where its pigment can be found, several leagues underground where there is no water at all.

Obviously I had struck a nerve, for I was suddenly spun and encased in swirls of translucent wind. A thundering below and a chasm opened. I dropped to my knees and beheld a maze of hollows harboring mounds of precious stones, golden bric-a-brac and parchment scrolls. It was the wondrous subterranean world that I had imagined as a child, with its elves and gnomes and the caves of Ali Baba. I was filled with happiness that such things truly existed. A joy swiftly followed by remorse. A stubborn cloud moved past the sun and the chill in the air lightened, then all was as it was. I stood before my worthy opponent waiting to be chastised.

—There are many truths and there are many worlds, said the sign solemnly.

—Yes, I said, feeling quite humbled. And you were right. I did dream, many dreams, and they were much more than dreams, as if originating from the dawn of mind. Yes, I absolutely dreamed.

The sign became very quiet. The palms ceased to bend, and a sweet silence enveloped the hill.

WHILE SITTING BENEATH the oversized letters spelling *coffee,* I met a couple who were driving to San Diego. I took this as an auspicious sign. An eight-hour drive, and I could ride along for eighty-five dollars. We arranged to meet in the morning. No talking was the rule. I hastily agreed, not really thinking anything of it.

That evening, though chilly, I walked the length of the Santa Cruz Wharf, the longest wooden pier in America, a half mile long. It was once used for shipping potatoes from San Francisco to the mining camps in the Sierra Nevada during the gold rush. Though normally lively, there was hardly a soul on the pier, no planes overhead, no vessels in sight, only the groans and wheezing of the sea lions sleeping.

I called Lenny, telling him I wasn't returning for a while. We talked of Sandy with heavy heart. We had all known one another so long. We met in 1971 after my first poetry performance, Lenny accompanying me on electric guitar. Sandy Pearlman was sitting cross-legged on the floor in St. Mark's Church, dressed in leather, Jim Morrison style. I had read his *Excerpts from the History of Los Angeles,* one of the greatest pieces written about rock music. After the performance, he told me I should front a rock 'n' roll band but I just laughed and told him I already had a good job working in a bookstore. Then he went on to reference Cerberus, the dog of Hades, recommending I delve into its history.

—Not just the history of a dog, but the history of an idea, he said, flashing his extremely white teeth.

I thought him arrogant, though in an appealing way, but his suggestion that I should front a rock band, though improbable, was also intriguing. At the time, I was seeing Sam Shepard and I told him what Sandy had said. Sam just looked at me intently and told me I could do anything. We were all young then, and that was the general idea. That we could do anything.

Sandy now unconscious at the ICU in Marin County. Sam negotiating the waxing phases of his affliction. I felt a cosmic pull in multiple directions and wondered if some idiosyncratic force field was shielding yet another field, one with a small orchard at its crux, heavy with a fruit containing an unfathomable core.

———

IN THE MORNING, I met the couple down the road. They were nothing if not unfriendly. I had to pour my coffee out by the curb so as not to spill any, then pay in advance before they would let me in the car, which was pretty beat up. The floor was littered with cans of mosquito repellent and moldering Tupperware, and the leather seats seemed to have been ripped open with a serrated knife. Various crime scenes passed through my mind, but their choice of music was great, tunes I hadn't heard for decades. After the sixth side, Charlie Gracie's *Butterfly,* I couldn't help myself.

—What a great playlist, I blurted.

To my surprise they suddenly pulled off to the side of the road. The guy got out and opened my door, giving me the nod.

—We said no talking. It's the cardinal rule.

—Please give me one more chance, I said.

Begrudgingly the guy started up the car and off we went. I wanted to ask if singing along was allowed, or gasping when a really great song came on, although so far, they were all great, from the extremely danceable to the mystically obscure. *Oh Donna. Summertime. Greetings (This Is Uncle Sam). My Hero. Endless Sleep.* I wondered if they were from Philly, the oldies city, it was that kind of music. I sat in dutiful silence, singing in my head, carried back to teenage dances and a boy named Butchy Magic, a blond Italian from South Philadelphia who seldom spoke but carried a switchblade, cruising across the landscape of homework into dreams to dwell in a silent chamber of a young, unrequited heart.

When we stopped for gas I took my sack and went to the bathroom, washed my face, brushed my teeth, got a coffee to go and returned in perfect silence just in time to see them speed off straight into the horizon of forgotten rhythm-and-blues songs. What the hell? Okay, then. *My Hero*, I yelled. That was great! Who plays *Endless Sleep* or *Greetings This Is Uncle Sam*? I stood there calling out an inventory of all the great songs I had savored in silence.

A security guard approached me.

—Is everything all right, miss?

—Oh yeah, sorry. I just missed my ride to San Diego.

—Hmmm. My daughter-in-law is driving to San Diego. I'm sure that if you share the gas money, she'll take you along.

Her name was Cammy, and she had a Lexus. I sat in the front seat. The back seat was loaded with boxes marked *Pickling* and a few marked *Avon*.

—The whole trunk is full of mason jars, she said. They're for a friend. She has an organic restaurant. I pickle everything for her. Onions, tomatoes, cucumbers, baby corn. She sells it in her restaurant. And I have a nice order for my relish in a place specializing in gourmet hot dogs.

Cammy was a fast driver, which was fine with me. She was also quite a talker, changing the radio station while talking, and then suddenly starting another conversation with the disembodied voice from the speaker. She wore tiny headphones and had a second phone charging. Cammy never stopped talking. She would ask a question, then answer it from her point of view. I hardly said a word. Still silent, but it was a different kind of silence. Finally I asked her if she heard anything about candy wrappers littering the beach near the OB Pier.

—No kidding, she said, that's so weird, they had the same thing happen in Redondo Beach, but not on the beach, actually in the back of the gasworks. Hundreds, maybe thousands of them. Crazy, right?

—Yeah, I said, though it didn't seem crazy. It seemed tactical.

—Did you hear about the missing kids?

—No, I said.

Her phone rang and she rattled off some ordering information, no doubt connected with her pickling empire.

—The whole world's going nuts, she continued. I was in Queens last spring and my sister's azalea bushes bloomed weeks ahead of time. Then out of nowhere there was a frost and they all died. I mean you can cover your plants with burlap if you get some warning, but it all happened overnight. All those dead flowers, she was heartbroken. And the squirrels in Central Park—did you hear about that? It was so warm they came out of hibernation, totally confused, and then it went ahead and snowed in April, on Easter no less. Snowing on Easter! Ten days later, the guys

WOW Café, OB Pier

that gather trash with those long picks found them. Scores of them, baby squirrels and their mothers, frozen to death. It's nuts, I tell you. The whole world is going nuts.

Cammy dropped me off on Newport Avenue by the Ocean Beach Pier, I gave her a fifty and she gave me a wink and took off. I checked into the old San Vicente Hotel, which hadn't changed much through the decades save in name. I was happy to be back in my same room on the second floor. Once I had imagined living in this room, cloaked in obscurity, writing detective stories. I opened the window and looked out at the long fishing pier with its lone café, a sight filling me with the pain of a welcomed nostalgia. It was a bit windy and the sound of the waves seemed to amplify the call of somewhere else, more surreal than real.

I rinsed my dirty clothes in the sink and hung them to dry in the shower, then grabbed my jacket and watch cap and took a quick turn on the beach. As I poked around I remembered that Cammy hadn't finished telling me about the missing kids. In any event there were no signs of a siege of wrappers, nothing unusual. I walked the length of the pier straight to the WOW Café. In the distance, I could see a pelican perched atop the seaward wall where *café* was written in huge blue letters. Another sight that filled me with the well-being of familiarity. People who make the coffee there are in touch with God. Their coffee doesn't hail from anywhere, not the beans of Kona, Costa Rica, or the Arabian fields. It's just coffee.

The WOW was unexpectedly full so I sat at the end of the common table, dominated by two guys who introduced themselves as Jesús and Ernest, and a blond pinup type who remained nameless. Jesús was from Santiago. I couldn't tell about Ernest, maybe Mexican, but maybe Russian; his eyes kept changing like a mood ring, from pure gray to the color of chocolate.

I found myself drawn to their conversation, which was centered on a string of recent hideous crimes, but after recognizing a few key markers I realized they were actually debating whether the murders in Sonoma in *The Part About the Crimes,* a section of Roberto Bolaño's masterwork *2666,* were real or fiction. At an impasse, they looked at me expectantly; after all, I had been eavesdropping for several minutes. Having read and reread the book I said that most likely the murders were real and the girls he described were symbolic of the real girls though not necessarily the actual girls. I mentioned I had heard that Bolaño had obtained a dossier concerning the unsolved murders of several young girls in Sonoma from a retired police detective.

—Yeah, I heard that too, Ernest said, though no one can be sure whether the story circulated about the police detective was real, or created in order to give credence to an imagined police report.

—Maybe they were exact descriptions from the police report but their names were changed, Jesús said.

—So, okay, let's say they were real, does being inserted by Bolaño within a work of fiction render them fiction? asked Ernest, peering at me with his changeling eyes.

I had a potential answer but said nothing. I was wondering what happens to the characters in books whose fates are left dangling by dying writers. The discussion petered out and I ordered chowder and biscuits. On the back of the menu was the history of the café. WOW stood for *walking on water*. I thought of miracles, of Sandy unresponsive. Why did I leave? I thought to stay near the hospital, keep vigil, coax a miracle, but didn't, dreading the deceptively antiseptic corridors and invisible bacterial zones, that trigger an instinct for self-survival and the overriding desire to flee.

Jesús and Ernest had picked up the pace again, talking simultaneously, sometimes lapsing into Spanish, and I missed out on the moment when the discussion shifted to the opening segment of *2666*, *The Part About the Critics*. Specifically, they were focused on the critics' dreams. One of an infinite and sinister swimming pool and the other of a body of living water.

—The writer must know his characters so well that he can access the content of their dreams, Ernest was saying.

—Who creates the dreams? asked Jesús.

—Well, who if not the writer?

—But does the writer create their dreams or does he channel the actual dreams of his characters?

—It's all about transparency, said Ernest. He sees through their skulls when they're sleeping. As if they were crystal.

The blonde stopped picking at her coleslaw and extracted a pack of cigarettes from her purse. They had a foreign look, a white pack with the words *Philip Morris* stamped in red. She placed the pack on the table next to a flip-top phone.

—Even more impressive is his unorthodox placement of space breaks, she said, inhaling deeply. *The water was alive*, he wrote, and then he places a space break. The reader is abandoned in the middle of a long, dark and infinite pool without so much as an inner tube.

We all stared at her mystified. Suddenly she seemed far more advanced than the rest of us. I was no longer hungry. Who would bring up a space break and thus end a conversation?

It was a good time to step out for air. I walked to the end of the pier, picturing Sandy in his baseball cap pulling into a parking spot in his white van, the one with the air of an intellectual hoarder, piled with books, dossiers, amplifier parts and obsolete computers. When he was young he had a sports car and we'd drive through Central Park, stopping at the Papaya King, or keep going all the way to the tip of Manhattan. Somewhere along the line he switched to his white van, and in the nineties, after a concert in Portland, we drove to Ashland to see a modern take of *Coriolanus* at the Oregon Shakespeare Festival. Sandy loved Shakespeare, especially *Midsummer Night's Dream*. The concept of transforming men into donkeys fascinated him. I told him that Carlo Collodi turned mischievous boys into double-crossed donkeys in *Pinocchio*. But the Bard did it first, he retorted triumphantly.

For some time, we plotted an opera based on Medea. Not the traditional opera that would require singers with a lifetime of training, but an opera nonetheless. He wanted me to play Medea. I told him I was too old to play her, but Sandy said Medea need only be formidable, and I was more than capable of negotiating the glare of her splintered mirror.

—Shards of love, Patti, he would say. Shards of love.

We talked endlessly of such things late at night searching for a place where he might get a slice of cheesecake. Our *Medea*. I wondered if we would ever write it. Though I guess in a way we had, in that van, under the stars shifting overhead.

Nothing had changed back at the table, though the subject had somehow switched to dog racing. The blonde had an ex-fiancé who owned no less than three champions in St. Petersburg.

—They have dog races in Russia?

—No, in Florida for Chrissakes.

—We should go. You can take a Greyhound from Burbank to Tampa.

—Yeah, with at least three transfers. But they're closing it all down, that's what I hear. It's bad news for the dogs, packs of highly skilled greyhounds out of work.

—There's no unemployment for racing dogs.

—They'll kill them off.

She pressed a hot paper towel against her eyelids to loosen the glue of her exceedingly long lashes.

—You could kill somebody with them lashes.

The blonde suddenly stood up. She was really something after all, a smart cookie with the curves of Jayne Mansfield.

Jesús and the blonde departed. Ernest pocketed the ball of tissue encasing the lashes. It seemed like he had something on his mind. He sat there for a few minutes spinning a dime on its edge, then he just picked up and left. I had the oddest feeling that Ernest wasn't really a stranger but I couldn't place him. I remained engrossed in penniless thoughts straight into sundown. Closing time, for the WOW had never been a nocturnal café.

MORNING LIGHT STREAMED across the thin coverlet. For a moment, I thought I was back at the Dream Motel. I was hungry and hurried down the stairs, passed some kids playing ball on the beach and trekked the length of the pier back to the WOW. I had fried eggs and beans, and was on my second cup of coffee deep in a Martin Beck mystery, *Murder at the Savoy*. Ernest had entered moccasin silent and parked himself across from me.

—*The Laughing Policeman* is better, he said.

—Yeah, I said, surprised to see him, but I already read it twice.

We sat and talked for a while. I couldn't help but marvel at our mutual ease winding from one obscure topic to another, from Swedish crime writers to extreme weather.

—What do you make of this? he asked.

A yellowed newspaper clipping from 2006. *Hurricane Ernesto Raises the Dead*. A photo of a small plot with overturned headstones.

—Was that in Virginia?

—It happened on an island off the Virginia coast. Same name as me.

—The island?

—No. The hurricane.

He carefully refolded the clipping and slipped it into a worn snakeskin wallet when a small black-and-white photograph dropped. I caught a glimpse of a woman in a dark flowered dress with a small boy. I wanted to ask him about it but he suddenly seemed uncomfortable. Instead I told him about the dream I had in Santa Cruz, the wrappers in the wrong colors, the bonfires at twilight and the enveloping sense of a strange chemical calm.

—Some dreams aren't dreams at all, just another angle of physical reality.

—How should I interpret that? I asked.

—The thing about dreams, Ernest was saying, is that equations are solved in an entirely unique way, laundry stiffens in the wind, and our dead mothers appear with their backs turned.

I just stared at him, wondering who he reminded me of.

—Look, he continued in a low voice, the bonfires haven't happened yet. You'll see them later on the beach exactly at twilight.

The sky was overcast, permeated by a strange illogical brightness. I tried to calculate the exact time of twilight. Most likely I would have looked it up on my phone if it wasn't dead. I removed my boots on the way back and walked barefoot in the frigid water. As a nonswimmer that's as far as I go. I thought about Sandy. I thought about Sam. I thought about Roberto Bolaño, only fifty years old, dying in a hospital instead of a cave off a rugged coast, or an apartment in Berlin, or his own bed.

Anticipating Ernest's appointed hour, I stayed close by. Through the arc of the afternoon I sat writing at the small white card table by the hotel window. There was a picture of my daughter between the pages of my notebook. She was smiling yet seemed on the verge of tears. I wrote of signs, strangers, yet nothing of my children though they were ever present. The sun was at its height. I felt myself surrendering, drawn by their abstract quiescence.

I awoke with a start. I couldn't believe I had fallen asleep again, sitting at a card table, no less. I quickly set up the ironing board, a portable one with a yellow oilcloth cover, unrolled the bottoms of my damp trousers, shook out the sand and ironed them dry, then hurried down the steps and crossed over to the beach. Dusk already, but I figured Ernest would still be there. Although maybe I had slept longer than I thought, for it appeared I had missed the action, no one was around, just a long row of small smoldering fires. I felt momentarily nauseous, as if I'd inhaled the smoke of the dead.

Two security guards suddenly appeared, accusing me of starting illegal bonfires. I found myself babbling, unable to answer their questions. For some reason, I couldn't remember what I was doing here, not just the scene of the fires, but here in the first place. I clawed through the fog. Sandy was in the hospital. We were going to the Dream Motel to write a segment for our *Medea,* the part where she falls into a trance and moves into the future, dressed in a black caftan with strings of massive amber beads carved with the heads of sacred birds.

—It's an opera, I was telling them, Medea removes her sandals and walks through the smoldering remains of the fires, one after another without a trace of emotion.

I could just live there for a while

They appeared as perplexed as I was. I was making a poor impression but couldn't assemble anything better. They gave a warning, lecturing on beach protocol, rules and fines. I hurried back to my room, cautioning myself not to look back. It was Ernest who had told me about the bonfires, a gathering at twilight. I knew that. Why didn't I speak up? I started thinking he had devised some kind of verbal trigger that temporarily closed a portal. The portal to him, that is. A pretty good device, I was thinking, but also quite tricky if used the wrong way. I tried to make out what the wrong way would be, but it was all too far-fetched. You're dreaming, I told myself, looking out at the long pier silhouetted by moonlight. At the same moment, I had a flash of the sign atop the hill shrouded in black mosquito netting.

Morning. First light, fading moon still visible. The rest of my clothes had dried so I folded them up, then sat by the window and finished *Murder at the Savoy*. Toward the end the widow of the cop killed in *The Laughing Policeman* sleeps with Detective Martin Beck in a hotel in Stockholm, something I never saw coming. Across the road gulls were competing over the remains of a sandwich; there were no signs of any bonfires on the beach.

Back at the WOW, I decided to put the whole bonfire thing out of mind and ordered coffee and cinnamon toast. The place was fairly empty and felt comfortably mine. I wished I could just live there for a while, in the WOW itself, in the back room with nothing but a simple cot, a

Greyhound terminal, Burbank

table to write on, an old refrigerator and an overhead fan. Every morning I'd make my coffee in a tin pot, rustle up some beans and eggs and read of the local occurrences in the newsletter. Just negotiating zones. No rules. No change. But then everything eventually changes. It's the way of the world. Cycles of death and resurrection, but not always in the way we imagine. For instance, we might all resurrect looking way different, wearing outfits we'd never be caught dead in.

Looking up from the hole I was perceptually burning, I spotted Ernest talking to Jesús, who seemed extremely agitated. Ernest rested his hand on his friend's shoulder and Jesús calmed, crossed himself and abruptly left. Ernest sat down and filled me in. Jesús and the blonde were heading to the Greyhound station in downtown Los Angeles, two days and nineteen hours on a bus to Miami, then a rent-a-car to St. Petersburg.

—Jesús seemed out of sorts.

—Muriel has a lot of luggage.

The blonde had a name.

—Did you return her lashes? I asked.

—A gull swooped down and took them, most likely they're part of a nest.

I avoided his gaze, so as not to catch him in a lie. In my mind's eye, I could see them quite plainly, without the slightest effort, wrapped in the same blob of tissue atop an old bureau beneath a painting of a lighthouse engulfed in badly executed mist. I noticed the book he'd set on the table, *Pascal's Arithmetical Triangle*.

—Are you reading that? I asked.

—You don't read books like this, you absorb them.

It made perfect sense to me, and I was certain he had a whole line of digressions planned, if only to divert me from the subject of bonfires, but I impulsively threw out my own line, just to shift the angles.

—You know, I was in Blanes some years back.

He looked at me quizzically: obviously he couldn't sense where I was going with this.

—Blanes?

— Yeah. It's a sixties-style beach town in Catalonia where Bolaño lived till his death. It's where he wrote *2666*.

Ernest was suddenly very serious. His love of Roberto Bolaño was something one could almost touch.

—It's hard to imagine what it must have been like for him, racing toward the finish line. He mastered the capacity that few can attain, like Faulkner or Proust or Stephen King, the ability to write and think simultaneously. The daily practice, he called it.

—The daily practice, I repeated.

—He laid it out in the opening pages of *The Third Reich*. Have you read it?

—I stopped reading midway, it made me uneasy.

—Why? he said, leaning in. What did you think was going to happen?

—I don't know, something bad, something bred of a misunderstanding about to go out of control, like in *The Prince and the Pauper.*

—You're talking dread.

—Yes, I suppose.

He glanced at my open notebook.

—Does your writing evoke that thing? That uneasiness?

—No. Except for maybe a comic uneasiness.

—*The Third Reich.* It's just the name of a board game. He was obsessed with them. A game is just a game.

—Yeah, I guess. You know, I have seen his games.

Ernest lit up like a pinball machine when everything goes the player's way.

—You have seen them? Bolaño's games!

—Yes, when I was in Blanes, I visited his family. The games were on a shelf in a closet. I took a photograph of them, though maybe I shouldn't have.

—Can I see the picture? he asked.

— Sure, I said. You can have it, but it may take me a while to find it.

He picked up his book, the one with a red and yellow cover heralding the triangle. He said he had somewhere to go, somewhere important. He wrote an address on the back of a napkin. We agreed to meet the following afternoon.

—And don't forget the picture.

Te Mana Café Voltaire Street. two o'clock. I folded the

napkin and motioned for another coffee. Unfortunately, I had impulsively promised to give the picture to him in spite of the fact it was somewhere in Manhattan and I hadn't the slightest notion where I had put it, what book I may have slipped it into, or what archival box I may have tossed it in, among hundreds of inconsequential shots. Black-and-white Polaroids of streets and architecture and the façades of hotels I thought I would always remember yet now were impossible to identify.

I didn't tell Ernest, but in truth, I'd had a sick feeling having accidently encountered Bolaño's games. Not bad sick but time-fracture sick. The closet shelf had contained a world of energy, the concentration once invested in those stacks of games still potent, manifesting as a hyper-objectified sense, observing every move I made.

The afternoon melted into evening. The moon rose, nearly full, affecting my bearings. I sat on the low cement wall watching the distant lights of the WOW go out. As though in answer the stars came out one by one, distant and ever present. It suddenly occurred to me that it wasn't really necessary that I be at the hospital with Sandy. For the past twenty years we have lived on opposite coasts, keeping channels open, trusting in the power of the mind to transcend three thousand miles. Why should anything be different? I could keep vigil wherever I may be, composing another kind of lullaby, one that would permeate sleep, one that would wake him up.

———

AS PROMISED, I met up with Ernest on Voltaire Street at a friendly Hawaiian-style joint that served pulled pork and smoothies with little umbrellas. He arrived late, already midsentence in a one-sided conversation and slightly disheveled, a button loosened on his shirt. Ernest ordered two Cuban-style coffees and excitedly laid out what was on his mind, the gist of it being that he was packing up and leaving, high on the trail of a saint who was delivering nutritionally deprived and afflicted children from lifestyle diseases.

—Do you have kids? I asked.

—No, he said, but the way I see it all children are our children. My sister has three kids. Two are so enormous they can hardly get around. She spoils them, and stuffs them with fried bread and sugar. The saint is going to save the children.

Questions were criss-crossing with everything I had read of the rise of pediatric cancers, diabetes and high blood pressure, the fast-food world closing in on our young.

—How will he do that? I asked.

—I can't tell you now.

—How do you know about him?

He stared at me intently, as if hoping I could hear his thoughts and save precious time.

—It came to me in a dream, like all sacred information.

He's in the desert and I think I know where to find him. It's a cult thing, a good one, and I'm joining. Maybe I can farm or help build shelters or arrange baseball teams for the boys.

—Girls play ball too.

—Yes of course, he said distractedly. Baseball for them all.

—Blessings on the children and thank you for trusting me.

—Maybe I'll see you there.

—But how would I find you? I asked.

—Keep the wrappers with you, put them under your pillow at night. It will come to you in your sleep. When you find the picture save it for me.

And then he was gone, on a mission anything but expected. There were starfish caught in multicolored nets adorning the walls. The coffee he ordered was sweet with a strong taste of cinnamon. I sat projecting myself back to New York sifting through layers of visual archaeology. To say nothing of the fact that the photograph was quite dark. The games had been neatly stacked, but nothing else was revealed of the closet's interior: his leather jacket, worn leather shoes, and his notebook for *2666*, slim, black with cryptic notations on graph paper. Things I saw and touched.

—That guy didn't pay his check, the waitress scolded.

—Oh, I'll take care of it, I said.

A button was on the floor by my foot. Just a small gray plastic button with a tiny thread attached, which I pocketed; a lucky penny heads-up from a dream within a dream.

That night I spread the wrappers on the table. No traces of chocolate. No candy smells. Aside from a bit of sand, clean as a whistle. *It's a cult thing,* Ernest had said. The absurdity of this investigation suddenly struck me and I laughed out loud. A laugh that hung in the air, as if to turn on me. I tried mapping it out. Okay, I was in the Dream Motel sitting in a chair by the sliding glass doors that led to the beach. I had a dream that propelled me to hitch from Santa Cruz to San Diego where I met Ernest who told me about the bonfires that no one saw save myself. I remember poking through charred wrappers and then folding bits of ash in a piece of gauze.

I leapt up and went through the pockets of my jacket, but the roll of gauze had vanished, though I noticed the tips of my fingers were smudged and blackened. Ernest had said to sleep with the wrappers under my pillow, but didn't indicate what state. In the bedside table drawer was a matchbook with a phone number written inside. Striking two heads at once I lit the wrapper. It burned slowly, letting off a faint scent of hayfields. I tore a page from my notebook, poured the ash in the center and folded it over and over, like an origami bird.

Slipping the packet under my pillow, I wondered if

Ernest and I were friends. After all, he knew nothing of me and I less of him. But it's like that sometimes, you can know an imperfect stranger like no one else. I noticed the gray button lying in the dust. I guess it fell out of my pocket when I threw off my jacket, still in a heap on the floor. I reached for the button, a small gesture identical to some other that I seemed destined to repeat.

There were hounds baying, and farther away, in Santa Cruz, the gutteral barking of the king of the sea lions reverberated over the wharf as the others slept. There was a low, whistling sound. The baying grew more and more faint. I could almost hear the prelude of *Parsifal* rising from an unworldly mist. A photograph fell from a wallet, a small boy with a woman in dark crepe. I was certain I had seen that image somewhere before, maybe a scene in a movie. A close-up of eyes the color of chocolate, an undulating carpet of tiny flowers that was no carpet at all, but the flounce of a dress illuminated by a passing car. I slipped my hand under the pillow and touched the packet, to be certain it was really there. Yes, I affirmed sleepily, then closed my eyes, enveloped by a hazy flutter of images: the swan and the spear and the Holy Fool.

BACK ON VOLTAIRE STREET I bumped into Cammy by the organic-food market and helped her deliver several cartons of onion jelly. I noticed her charger plugged into her dashboard. My phone was long dead as I had left my charger at the Dream Motel, dangling in the wall socket, sadly without purpose. Cammy let me use her cell phone so I could check about Sandy. She talked through the entire phone call but I managed to grasp the report. He had not regained consciousness.

She was telling me she had met a woman who knew the uncle of one of the missing kids she had mentioned at the end of our drive. I had almost forgotten. It turned out the boy was returned unharmed with a tag pinned to his shirt saying that he had a heart murmur. Never diagnosed but swiftly confirmed. He cried all night, wanting to go back, refusing to tell them anything. I said nothing but could not help thinking it was very close to the story of the crippled boy who was sent back home after a brief taste of paradise in the tale of the Pied Piper.

—I have to go to Los Angeles tomorrow, she told me. I have a big delivery in Burbank.

—I was thinking of going to Venice Beach, I said impulsively, mind if I come along? I'll pay for the gas.

—Done deal, she said.

That night I used the hotel phone and called everyone I thought I should call. Not one person was in, or rather, not one person answered. I left messages. *My phone is dead. I'm fine. You can call at the hotel.* There was something funereal about the whole episode. Four people, four dead phones. I closed the window. It was getting chilly. I picked up the hotel pen and filled a few pages of my notebook waiting for the phone to ring, but it didn't.

I checked out and had a stale bran muffin and black coffee in the lobby. Cammy pulled up in her Lexus. She was wearing a pink sweater and the back seat was loaded with taped-up cartons. As we drew closer to Los Angeles, she brought me up to speed about the various comings and goings in Cammy world, some of which I mercifully missed out on as my mind was elsewhere.

—Oh goodness, she blurted, did you hear about the disappearances in Macon?

—Macon, Georgia? Are you talking about children?

—Yep, seven kids.

I experienced that kind of feeling I get when looking down from an extremely high place. It was as if tiny ice cells were moving slowly, vibrating in my veins.

—Can you believe that? she said. One of the biggest Amber Alerts ever.

Cammy switched on the radio but there was nothing about it in the news. Both of us fell into a welcomed silence until she pulled into Venice. I gave her forty dollars and she gave me a small mason jar labeled *rhubarb and strawberry jam*.

—Seven children, I said numbly, undoing my seatbelt.

—Yeah, she said, can you believe that? It's nuts. Nothing was posted, nothing was demanded. It was like they were just spirited away by the Pied Piper himself.

VENICE BEACH, city of detectives. Where there's a palm tree, there's Jack Lord, there's Horatio Caine. I checked in at a small hotel near Ozone Avenue, not far from the board-walk. From my window, I could see the young palms and the back entrance of the On the Waterfront Café, a good place for lunch. The coffee arrived in a white mug deco-rated with an engaging blue starfish floating above their motto—*Where the Brew Is as Good as the View*. The tables were covered with dark green oilcloth. I had to keep swat-ting flies away, but that didn't bother me. Nothing bothered me, not even the things that bothered me.

I noticed across from me a good-looking fellow like a young Russell Crowe sitting across from a girl with a lot of pancake makeup. Probably covering bad skin, but she had an inner thing you could feel across the room, deco-rated with dark glasses, dark bob, fake leopard coat, a born replica of a movie star. They were immersed in their world and I in theirs, imagining them as detective Mike Hammer and the glamorously detached Velda. While I was writing this all down, the pair left unobserved, their table cleared and new napkins and clean utensils laid, as if they had never been there.

I always liked the beach in Venice as it seems vast, a wide expanse that increases at low tide. I removed my boots, rolled up my pants and walked along the shore.

The water was extremely cold but therapeutic, my sleeves soaked from scooping up seawater to splash on my face and neck. I noticed a single wrapper caught up in the waves but didn't retrieve it.

The trouble with dreaming, a familiar voice trailed, but I was lured away by the sound of peculiar birds, big squawky ones, standing at attention and right on the verge of speaking. Unfortunately, a small part of me was already debating whether birds could actually speak, which broke the connection. I circled back, questioning myself why I had regrettably hesitated when I am well aware that certain winged creatures possess the ability to form words, spin monologues and at times dominate an entire conversation.

I decided on the Waterfront for dinner but went the opposite way and passed a wall covered in murals, Chagall-like scenes from *Fiddler on the Roof*, floating violinists amidst tongues of flame that produced a disconcerting sense of nostalgia. When I finally circled back and entered the Waterfront, I thought I had made a mistake. The layout looked totally different than in the afternoon. There was a pool table and nothing but fellas of all ages with baseball caps and huge glasses of beer with slices of lemon. Several looked at me as I entered, an unthreatening alien, then went about the business of drinking and talking. There was a hockey game on a big screen with no sound. The din, the drone, was all male, amiable male, laughing and talking, broken only by the tapping of a ball with a cue stick, the ball dropping into the pocket. I ordered coffee, a fish sandwich and salad, the most expensive plate on the menu. The fish was small and deep-fried, but the lettuce and onions were fresh. The same starfish mug, the same brew. I laid my money on the table and went out. It was raining. I put on my watch cap. Passing the mural, I nodded to the Yiddish fiddler, commiserating an unspoken fear of friends slipping away.

The heat wasn't working in my room. I laid on the couch, bundled up, half watching the *Extreme Homes* channel, endless episodes featuring architects outlining how they built into rock and sloping shale or the mechanics of realizing a five-ton revolving copper roof. Dwelling places that resembled huge boulders replicating real surrounding boulders. Houses in Tokyo, Vail and the California desert. I would fall asleep and open my eyes to a repeat of the same Japanese house, or a house that represented the three parts of *The Divine Comedy*. I wondered what it would feel like to sleep in a room manifesting Dante's Hell.

In the morning, I watched the gulls swooping by my window. It was closed, so I could not hear them. Silent, silent gulls. There was a light rain and the hair of the high palms swayed in the wind. I put on my cap and jacket and went looking for breakfast. With the Waterfront closed, I settled for a place on Rose Avenue that had its own bakery and a vegetarian menu. I got a bowl of kale and yams, but what I really wanted was steak and eggs. The guy next to me was chattering away to his partner about some country that was importing giant carnivorous snapping turtles to get rid of the corpses floating in a sacred river.

There was a used-book store off Rose. I looked for a copy of *The Third Reich* but there were no books by Bolaño. I found a secondhand DVD of *The Pied Piper,* starring Van Johnson. I couldn't believe my luck. I could hear Kay Starr, the mother of the crippled boy, singing her poignant lament. *Where's my son, my son John?* Which got me thinking of the missing children. Kids and candy wrappers. They had to be related, though maybe not in the same proximity. Incredibly, there wasn't a word about the missing kids in any of the papers. I was having my doubts about the whole thing, though it was hard to believe Cammy would make up such a story.

I walked through an arcade on Pacific, stopping at a door that said *Mao's Kitchen*. I stood there wondering if I should enter when the door opened and a woman motioned for me to come in. It was a communal kind of place, with an open kitchen fitted with industrial stoves and pots of steaming dumplings beneath a sign that said *The People's Grub* along with faded posters of rice fields on the back wall. I was reminded of a past journey when my friend Ray and I went looking for the cave near the Chinese border where Ho Chi Minh wrote the Vietnamese Declaration of Independence. We walked through endless rice paddies, pale gold, and the sky a clear blue, staggered by what was an ordinary spectacle for most. The woman brought a pot of fresh ginger, lemon and honey.

—You were coughing, she said.

—I'm always coughing, I laughed.

There was a fortune cookie on my saucer. I slipped it in my pocket to save for later. I felt connected to the modest peace offered with the fare, thinking about nothing. Just wisps of things, meaningless things, like remembering my mother once told me that Van Johnson always wore red socks, even in black and white movies. I wondered if he wore them when he played the Piper.

Back in my room I opened the cookie and unwound the fortune. *You will step on the soul of many countries.* I'll be careful, I said under my breath, but upon second glance I realized it actually said *soil*. In the morning, I decided to retrace my steps, go back to the beginning, return to the same city to the same hotel in Japantown steps away from the same Peace Tower. It was time to sit vigilance with Sandy, clawing his way through cellular extremes—not, as was his custom, to explore an imagined system, but to plumb the depths of himself. On the way to the airport it occurred to me that the Pied Piper story was not essentially one of revenge but of love. I got a one-way ticket to San Francisco. For a moment, I thought I saw Ernest passing through security.

Peace Tower, Japantown

ICU

The traffic was light reentering San Francisco. My room at the Miyako Hotel wasn't ready so I passed through two internal malls and ate at On the Bridge. Everything was just as it had been only weeks before, though I missed Lenny's reassuring presence. The cook made me flying-fish-roe spaghetti. Anime clips from *Dragon Ball* were looping on the TV screens. I found myself plowing through the trajectory of manga, flipping backwards through *Death Note 7*, trying to make sense of the graphics: a black menace hovering over the boy Light sifting through pages of intermittent numerical sequences. My spaghetti was gone. I hardly recalled eating it. The check was dated February 1. Where had January flown? I made a list of things I should have been doing. I'll do them soon, I told myself, but first thing in the morning, I would go to the hospital where Sandy remained unconscious in the Intensive Care Unit. In spite of that fact, I stopped at a small shop and bought him some sweets made with red bean paste. Sandy loved such things, fan-shaped bits of heaven.

I turned in early. There was nothing on TV. I imagined I was in Kyoto, which wasn't hard as the hotel bed was close to the floor next to a rice-paper lamp and a tableau of grayscale pebbles studiously arranged in a bamboo sandbox. There was a candy-striped pencil on the nightstand. I'm not so sleepy, I told myself, I should get up and write, but I didn't. In the end, I wrote the words that are here, even as a whole other set of words slipped away, *alphabeting* the ether, taunting me in my sleep. *You don't follow plots you negotiate them.* Manga guidance, a repetitive mantra melding with my own thoughts.

The pencil seemed far away, well beyond my grasp, and I actually watched myself fall asleep. The clouds were pink and dropped from the sky. I was wearing sandals, kicking through mounds of red leaves surrounding a shrine on a small hill. There was a small cemetery with rows of monkey deities, some adorned with red capes and knitted caps. Massive crows were picking through the drying leaves. *It doesn't mean anything,* someone was shouting, and that was all I could remember.

In the morning, I arranged transportation to the hospital in Marin County helped by mutual friends who had taken it upon themselves to tend to Sandy. With no living family, the task was left to this small devoted circle who knew and loved him. I reentered the ICU. Nothing had changed since my last visit with Lenny; the doctor seemed to have little hope of Sandy regaining consciousness. I circled his bed. A hospital chart was tacked to the foot, his middle name was Clarke, my son was born on his birthday, a fact I had somehow forgotten. I stood there scrambling for the right thoughts, ones that could permeate the coma's thick veil. I had flashes of Arthur Lee in prison, little red books spread out like a pack of cards. I could see Sandy falling in slow motion in a parking lot near an ATM. I could almost hear him thinking. *Convalescence. Latin. Fifteenth century.* I stayed for as long as I could, doing my best to suppress my intense phobia of tubes, syringes and the artificial silence of hospital settings.

I shuttled back and forth from hotel to hospital. The medicinal smells and rubber-soled entrances of the nurses with clipboards and plastic bags of fluids unnerved me as I sat bedside desperately searching for a way in, some connective channel. On my last day, though visiting hours had ended, no one instructed me to leave so I stayed until nightfall. I found myself projecting constellations of words onto his white sheets, an endless jumble of phrases streaming from the mouths of miraculous totems lining an inaccessible horizon. Medea and monkey gods and kids and candy wrappers. What do you make of it, Sandy? I prodded silently. Machines pulsing. Saline solution dripping. Sandy squeezed my hand but the nurse said it didn't mean anything.

Hie Shrine

There was a shipping place directly across from the hotel. I packed up the last of my belongings and sent them to New York, then walked to the other end of town toward Jack Kerouac territory. Passing through Chinatown, I collided unexpectedly with preparations for the lunar new year, the Year of the Monkey. Bits of colored paper fell from the sky, small squares with a monkey face stamped in red. *Parade 27*. It was certain to be spectacular but I'd be long gone by then. Funny how I left San Francisco on one new year and was leaving again on another. I could feel the gravitational pull of home, which when I'm home too long becomes the gravitational pull of somewhere else.

The bench of the three wise monkeys was empty. I sat for a few minutes composing myself as the festivities took me by surprise. I remembered as a child standing before a similar effigy of the three monkeys in a park with my uncle. Which monkey would you rather be? he asked. The one that sees, speaks or hears no evil? I felt vaguely sick, afraid of making the wrong choice.

I found a side street just off the perimeter. Dumplings to go, two tables covered with yellow oilcloth. No menu. I sat and waited. A round-faced boy in pajamas appeared with a glass of tea and a small basket of steamed dumplings, then disappeared behind a pink-and-green floral curtain. I sat for some time wondering what to do next, finally deciding to follow whatever impulse dominated other impulses. In other words, whatever impulse won. The tea was cold and I was suddenly conscious of being isolated in a strange eatery. This exaggerated sensation escalated until I felt as if I was held within a force field, like an inhabitant in the bottled city of Kandor in an old *Superman* comic.

I could hear strings of firecrackers going off a few streets away. The Year of the Monkey had begun and I wasn't at all sure how it would play out. My mother was born in 1920, the Year of the Metal Monkey, so I reasoned her blood might protect me. The boy failed to return so I left some money on the table, slipped through the invisible barrier and walked from Chinatown to Japantown, back to the hotel.

I spread my few possessions on the bed: my camera with crushed bellows, identity card, notebook, pen, dead phone and some money. I decided to go home soon but not just yet. I used the hotel phone and called the poet who'd given me a black coat, a beloved coat that I had lost.

—Can I visit for a while, Ray?

—Sure, he said without hesitation, you can sleep in my café. I'm making green coffee.

I had a Japanese-style breakfast in an oblong lacquer box, then checked out. The old valet who had been stationed there for years asked me when I was coming back.

—Soon, I guess, when I have another job.

—It's going to be different, he said mournfully. No more Japanese rooms.

—But this has always been a Japanese-style hotel, I protested.

—Things change, he was saying as I slid into the cab.

The flight to Tucson was two hours and eleven minutes. Ray was waiting when I disembarked.

—Where have you been? he said.

—Oh, around. Santa Cruz. San Diego. Where were you?

—Buying coffee in Guatemala. Then in the desert. I tried calling you, he said, narrowing his eyes.

—I didn't get the message, I said somewhat apologetically. My phone's been dead for quite a while, actually.

—Not that kind of message, he said.

—Oh yeah, I laughed. Well, I'm here, so I guess I got it.

He closed up the café, made us soup with corn and yucca, then unrolled a mat and made a bed for me. We had known each other a long time, had together traveled to hard places and could easily adapt to each other's routines. He provided me with a work table and a child's lamp with a waterfall painted on the skin of the shade that seemed to flow when you turned on the light. Late at night we listened to Maria Callas and Alan Hovhaness and Pavement. He played chess on his computer as I scanned the books lining his shelves, among them the *Cantos* of Pound, the collected works of Rudolf Steiner and a thick volume on Euclidean geometry, which I removed. It was a heavily illustrated book that I couldn't begin to understand, but attempted to absorb.

—I lost your coat, I told him. The black one you gave me on my birthday.

—It will come back, he said.

—What if it doesn't?

—Then it will greet you in the afterlife.

I smiled, feeling strangely reassured. I didn't mention the candy wrappers or the missing kids or Ernest. It seemed as if I had already shed the skin of those days. We did talk of Sandy, though, and of many friends gone yet animated through mutual sentiment. After a few days, he had to leave. I don't know when I'll be back, he said, but stay as long as you like. He charged my phone and showed me how to use his shortwave radio. I messed with it for a while and tuned in the Grateful Dead channel.

It was still dark and Jerry was singing *Palm Sunday*. I was cold and searched the closet for a blanket. I found an off-white Pendleton, and when I shook it out something fell from a fold. As I bent down to pick it up, a shaft of moonlight shot through the window. It was a crumpled wrapper, Peanut Chewz, the wrong color, *chews* misspelled, no chocolate residue. Curious, I searched the closet for another and found a cardboard box loosely sealed with packing tape. An entire carton of pristine wrappers, hundreds of them. I pocketed a few, retaped the box and went outside to look at the moon, a large bright pie in the sky.

I went over our conversation. *I tried to call you.* I knew that he had. It was the psychic nature of our way. I thought back to the places we had traveled to: Havana, Kingston, Cambodia, Christmas Island, Vietnam. We had found Lenin Stream, where Ho Chi Minh washed. In Phnom Penh, leeches covered me when we were trapped in the flooding streets. I stood by the sink in the hotel bathroom and shuddered while Ray calmly picked them off. I remembered a baby elephant decorated with flowers emerging from the dense jungle in Angkor Wat. I had my camera and slipped away to follow it on my own. When I returned I found him sitting on the wide veranda of a temple, surrounded by children. He was singing to them, the sun a halo around his long hair. I could not help but think of the scripture—*Suffer the little children to come unto me.* He looked up at me and smiled. I heard laughter, tinkling bells, bare feet on the temple stairs. It was all so close, the rays of the sun, the sweetness, a sense of time lost forever.

———

IN THE MORNING, I drank two glasses of mineral water, scrambled some eggs with green onions and ate standing up. I counted my money, pocketed a map, filled a water bottle and wrapped some buns in a cloth. It was the Year of the Monkey and I had beamed down into a new territory, on a road without shadow beneath the molecular sun. I kept walking, figuring I'd eventually hitch a ride. I shaded my eyes and saw him coming. He rolled down the window of a beat blue Ford pickup, a chunk of old sky transfigured. He had a different shirt on, with all buttons intact, and in a way seemed like someone else, someone I once knew.

—You're not a hologram, are you? I asked.

—Get in, said Ernest. We'll drive through the desert. There's a place I know that has the best huevos rancheros, and coffee that you can actually drink with pleasure. Then you can judge whether I'm a hologram or not.

There was a rosary wrapped around the rearview mirror. It felt familiar driving with Ernest in the middle of the unexplained; dream or no dream, we had already crisscrossed some curious territory. I trusted his hands on the wheel. They evoked other hands, those of good men.

—Ever hear of a muffler? I said.

—It's an old truck, he replied.

Ernest did most of the talking. Metaphysical geometry, in his low, meditative style, as if he was drawing words from a secret compartment. I rolled down the window. Endless scrub dotted with supplicating cacti.

—There's no hierarchy. That's the miracle of a triangle. No top, no bottom, no taking sides. Take away the tags of the Trinity—Father, Son and Holy Spirit—and replace each with love. See what I mean? Love. Love. Love. Equal weight encompassing the whole of our so-called spiritual existence.

We were heading west. Ernest pulled into a small outpost with a gas pump, some souvenirs and a small eatery. A woman came out and greeted him like an old friend, then served us coffee and two plates of huevos rancheros with refried beans and a silky mash of avocado. A paint-by-numbers oil of Our Lady of Guadalupe was tacked to the wall next to a faded photograph of Frida Kahlo and Trotsky in a tin frame.

—My granddaughter painted it, she said, wiping her hands on her apron.

It was pretty bad but who could fault a child?

—It's very nice, I told her.

Ernest looked at me from across the table.

—Well? he said expectantly.

—Well what?

—You weren't listening. You were somewhere else.

—Oh, sorry.

— So, he continued, moving the last of his beans around with his fork, are they the best huevos you've ever had?

Love. Love. Love.

Outpost, Salton Sea

—They're really good, I said, but I may have had better.

—I'm listening, he said, vaguely irritated.

—In Acapulco in 1972. I was a guest in a villa over-looking the sea. I don't know how to swim and there was a big pool, quite deep. Another guest taught me how to float on my back, which seemed quite an accomplishment at the time.

—Swimming is overrated, he said.

—One morning I got up before breakfast, stepped down into the pool and floated. I closed my eyes for the sun was already quite bright, and I felt free and content, but when I opened my eyes, there were hawks circling above me.

—How many?

—I don't know. Maybe three, maybe five, but it seems to me they had red tails. They were beautiful, but too close, and I wondered if they thought I was dead and I panicked. The clouds moved and the sun illuminated their wings, and I was flailing and I really thought I was going to drown. Suddenly there was a huge splash. The cook jumped in and grabbed me around the waist, lifted me above the water, pulled me out and pushed the water out of my lungs. Then he dried me off and made me huevos rancheros, the best I ever had.

—Did that really happen?

—Yes, I said, with absolutely no embellishment, I still dream of it. But it was not a dream.

—What was his name?

—He was the cook. I don't remember his name but I've never forgotten him. I can see his face in many faces. He was the cook and wore white and he saved my life.

—Where do you actually come from?

—Why, I laughed, are you going to drive me home?

—Anything is possible, he said. After all, it's the Year of the Monkey.

He laid some money down and we walked outside. I finished my coffee, then got back in the truck while he checked a tire. I was about to ask him what his take was on the new lunar year when I noticed the sun had shifted. We drove awhile in silence as the sky turned a brilliant rose with streaks of ruby and violet.

—The trouble with dreaming, he was saying, but I was a world away tramping the red earth in the heart of the Northern Territory.

—You need to go there, he said adamantly.

—Actually, I said, somewhat startled, what I really need is a bathroom.

There were no facilities around. I should have gone before but I seemed to remember an out-of-order sign on the restroom door. We were in the middle of a rock-and-scruff-covered plain. Somewhat arid, somewhat like the moon. Ernest pulled off the road and we just sat there. The pressure was on. Grabbing my sack, I walked well out of range and squatted behind a cluster of silvery cacti. A long trail of urine slid across the baked earth. I was mulling over the fact that Ernest somehow knew I was thinking about Ayers Rock. I thought of Sam and how years back we often dreamed the same dream, and how he seems, even now, to know what I'm thinking. The trail completely dried up and a tiny lizard scurried across my boot. Shaking myself back into the immediate, I rose and zipped up, then headed back to the truck. Strewn across the dead terrain were carcasses of small fish, hundreds of them, thousands maybe, curling in on themselves, like salt-encrusted candy wrappers. Approaching, I saw nothing but exit dust. Ernest had left. I stood very still, surveying the situation, thinking that's all right, it's as good a place as any to get lost in, the surrounds of the Salton Sea, that is no sea at all.

It seemed as if I walked for miles, yet everything stayed the same. I was sure that I had covered a lot of ground, but wasn't getting anywhere. I tried speeding up, then slowing down, figuring I'd collide with myself and break the loop, but no such luck, the long desert panorama kept readjusting itself, until any new routine became a loop in itself. I pulled a stale bun wrapped in a napkin out of my pocket. It was dusted in sugar and tasted faintly of oranges, like one of those Day of the Dead cakes. I got to thinking about the boys in the diner, wondering if their conversation was mere coincidence and if my assessment of *candy wrapper* as a noun was actually correct. I also wondered if the mundanity of my train of thought was hindering my progress.

I switched to a mental dart game, a revolving target of time-altering possibilities that Sandy and I would play on long drives. I released a dart that lit all the way to Flanders at the close of the Middle Ages, prompting me to assault the air with new queries, such as why the gilded phrase of the young Virgin, swathed in robes, reads from right to left and also downwards on the Annunciation panel of the *Ghent Altarpiece*. Might it be that the painter was merely toying with us? Or was the imperceptible balloon encasing her words upside down and backwards simply to accommodate the eye of the Holy Spirit, translucent and winged, positioned above her?

This preoccupation gradually eclipsed any concerns of nouns and verbs or my whereabouts as I fluidly revisited the historical past. I saw the hand of the master painter closing the outer wings of the panels. I saw other hands reverently opening the same panels. Their wooden frames were dark from the deepening of time. I saw thieves carrying the panels away to a ship that sailed into treacherous seas. I saw the battered hull and the broken mast. The sky was pale blue without a single cloud and I kept walking, drinking slowly, carefully measuring my water supply. I walked until I was where I wanted to be, before the dove and the maiden, the fat of the lamb melting away.

St. Jerome's study, Albrecht Dürer

WHAT MARCUS SAID

Traveling west to east across time zones is harder to negotiate than when reversed. Something about pacemaker cells. Not a reference to an artificial device but the portion of the mind that keeps us bodily in sync. Some weeks on the West Coast had definitely toyed with my P-cells. Groggy at dinner, then nodding, and waking at 2 a.m. I took to night walking, bundled in silence. With an absence of traffic, there was a relatable deadness in the air. Back home, in the center of February, the forgotten month.

Valentine's Day was the coldest on record in New York City's history. A complex mantle of frost covered everything, bare branches strung with a symphony of frozen hearts. Pendants of ice, lethal enough to wound, cracked and plummeted from the edges of the overhangs and scaffolding onto the sidewalks, left to lie like discarded weapons of a primitive age.

I wrote very little, nor did I commune within the dreamer's dream. Across America one light after another seemed to burn out. The oil lamps of another age flickered and died. The sign was silent, but the books on my night table beckoned. *The Children's Crusade*. *The Colossus*. Marcus Aurelius. I opened his *Meditations: Do not act as if you had ten thousand years to live* . . . This made terrible sense to me, climbing the chronological ladder, approaching my seventieth year. Get a grip, I told myself, just revel in the last seasons of being sixty-nine, the sacred Jimi Hendrix number, with his answer to such a caution: *I'm going to live my life the way I want to*. I imagined Marcus and Jimi clashing, each choosing a massive icicle that would melt in their hands long before they acquiesced to spar.

The cat was rubbing against my knee. I opened a can of sardines, chopped up her share, then cut some onions, toasted two slices of oat bread and made myself a sandwich. Staring at my image on the mercurial surface of the toaster, I noticed I looked young and old simultaneously. I ate hastily, failing to clean up, actually craving some small sign of life, an army of ants dragging crumbs dislodged from the cracks of the kitchen tiles. I longed for buds sprouting, doves cooing, darkness lifting, spring returning.

Marcus Aurelius asks us to note the passing of time with open eyes. Ten thousand years or ten thousand days, nothing can stop time, or change the fact that I would be turning seventy in the Year of the Monkey. Seventy. Merely a number but one indicating the passing of a significant percentage of the allotted sand in an egg timer, with oneself the darn egg. The grains pour and I find myself missing the dead more than usual. I notice that I cry more when watching television, triggered by romance, a retiring detective shot in the back while staring into the sea, a weary father lifting his infant from a crib. I notice that my own tears burn my eyes, that I am no longer a fast runner and that my sense of time seems to be accelerating.

I do what I can to augment this recurring image in my favor, even replacing the egg timer with a crystal hourglass passing the dust of ground marble, such as the type found in the small wooden study of St. Jerome or the workshop of Albrecht Dürer. Even as there is most likely some finite principle concerning the rate that sand passes through an hourglass, no advantage in having a stately glass or more perfect grains.

Since contemplating Marcus, I try to be more aware of the passing hours, that I might see it happen, that cosmic shift from one digit to another. Despite all efforts February just slips away, though being a leap year there is one extra day to observe. I stare at the number 29 on the daily calendar, then reluctantly tear off the page. March first. My wedding anniversary, twenty years without him, which prompts me to pull an oblong box from under the bed, opening the lid long enough to smooth the folds of a Victorian dress partially obscured by a fragile veil. Sliding the box back into its place I feel strangely off-center, a moment of sorrow's vertigo.

In the outer world, the sky had fast darkened, high winds moved in from four directions, churning in concert with a rapid onset of torrential rains, and just like that, everything broke. It happened so quickly that I had no time to retrieve clothes and books from the floor or seal up my compromised skylight, water rushing everywhere, surging above the ankles, then up to my knees. The door seemingly disappeared and I was trapped in the center of my room when an elliptical blackness, a widening aperture, taking up much of the plaster wall, opened onto a lengthy path strewn with dark toys. Wading toward it I saw errant tops zigzagging through a narrow lea of daffodils, mowing them down, tossing their trumpet shapes into the unstable air. I reached out, blindly seeking a way out or way into the void, when a chorus of birdlike cries startled me.

—Just a game, a playful voice twittered.

There was no mistaking the supercilious tones of the sign. I backed away, marshalling my courage.

—Very well, I retorted, but which game?

—The Game of Havoc, of course.

I knew something of this so-called game. Havoc, an uppercase game with a lowercase deity, spelling nothing but trouble for the unwary participant. One finds himself assailed with components of a dreadful equation. One evil eye, two spinning stars, perpetually winding gears.

Unequivocal havoc instigated by the current lunar god and his band of winged monkeys, a pervasive lot who once preyed upon the unsuspecting Dorothy in the hypnotic fields of Oz.

—I think I'll pass, I said adamantly, and as swiftly as it all began, it abruptly ended.

I assessed the damage. Save for a bit of a mess all was as it was. Confronted with sudden calm, I inspected the length of the wall: not the slightest trace of an oval access, not a ripple, the plaster was completely smooth. I ran my hand across the finish, imaging frescoes, a bustling studio lined with vats of glittering pigments, a sky of Prussian blue, yellow ochre and crimson lake. I once yearned to exist in such times, a young girl with a muslin cap gazing at Goethe's color wheel, bright and obscure, turning slowly beneath the surface of a mercury pool. Momentarily retracing its source, I noted that the narcissus of spring had budded too early, then watched as it shivered and recoiled.

Water dripped from the unsecured section of the skylight. Severed blooms everywhere, releasing an anesthetizing scent when crushed underfoot. Shrugging off any drowsing effect, I tossed the yellow heads into the dustbin, got out the mop and bucket and wiped down the wood floors. Afterwards I set about the task of separating several waterlogged pages of a scattered manuscript, dismayed to watch words dissolve into indecipherable smears.

—The pool is also a mirror, I said aloud, to whoever might be listening.

I sat on the edge of the bed, took some deep breaths and slipped on some dry socks. The coming days of March taunted me. The death of Artaud. Robert Mapplethorpe's passing. The birth of Robin, and my mother's birthday, on the same day the swallows are said to return to Capistrano, followed by the first day of spring. My mother. How I sometimes longed to hear her voice. I wondered if her swallows would return this year, a child's query revisited.

March winds. March wedding. The Ides of March. Josephine March. Numinous March with its strong associations. And of course, there has always been the March Hare. I remember as a child being quite taken with the quirky Hare, sure that he and the Mad Hatter were one and the same, even sharing the same initials. I held to the idea that they were transposable and yet could remain themselves. Rational adults thought this improvable, yet I could not be argued down, not by a Tenniel illustration or Disney cartoon, not even by Lewis Carroll himself. My logic may have been full of holes but so was Wonderland. The Hare presided over an endless tea party, as calculable time had been slain long before the party began. It was the Hatter who did the slaying, spreading his arms and singing the immutable Wonderland theme, one that I listened for intently throughout my childhood. When Johnny Depp embraced the role of the Hatter he too was drawn into this multiplicity of being and ceased to be just Johnny. Without a doubt, he became the harbinger of this hallowed little song.

—Will we die a little? he sang, extending his arms as if to encompass all. I heard this with my own ears as each note plopped like a joyous tear, then dissipated. Since then I have often considered the bidding of Johnny's Hatter— *Will we die a little?* What could he have meant? A blameless bit of topsy-turvy, no doubt, or a kind of homeopathic spell, a small death immunizing against the terrors of the greater one.

The first hours of March melted into the days that followed. I let myself be led, no more than a droplet sliding down the spiraled tail of the monkey. On my mother's birthday, it was reported that the swallows had indeed found their way back to Capistrano. That night I dreamt that I was back in San Francisco at the Miyako Hotel. I was standing in the center of a Zen garden that was not much more than a glorified sandbox, and I heard my mother's voice. Patricia, was all she said.

On the first day of spring I shook out the feather bed and opened the shutters. Virtual lockets were falling from the branches of young trees and the numbing fragrance of the narcissus returned. I commenced with my chores, whistling an oft-forgotten tune, certain that we, as the seasons, prevail and that ten thousand years is yet a blink in the eye of a ringed planet or that of an archangel armed with a sword of glass.

Sam's Stetson

BIG RED

April Fool's Day. A trickster grappled with the reins of action, as balls of confusion rolled toward us, scores of steely shooters, tripping us up, keeping us off-balance. The news pounded, and minds raced to make sense of the campaign of a candidate compounding lies at such a speed that one could not keep up, or break down. The world twisted at his liking, poured over with a metallic substance, fool's gold, already peeling away. Rain and more rain, April showers, just like the nursery rhyme, it fell straight across America, to the west, over Marin County, a melancholy witness to Sandy's struggles. I tried to shrug off unease, do my work, say my prayers, bide my time. More rain pelted the skylight, a thousand erratic hoofbeats, munificent energies racing toward earth.

I sat at my desk and opened my computer, slowly wading through a long chain of requests. There were plenty of them, mostly work-related, and I set about the task of considering each potential job, stopping excitedly somewhere in the middle. I was offered work in Australia, in a year's time, concerts in Sydney, Melbourne and a festival in Brisbane. I closed my computer, pulled out an atlas and turned to a map of Australia. It was quite a trek and a long time away, but I knew exactly what I would do, perform nine concerts and then, with the band gone home, hop on a prop plane to Alice Springs and hire a driver to take me to Uluru. I answered immediately. Yes, I will do the work, and marked the days in the 2017 calendar, which was completely empty. Several *A*s across the following March, Australia to Ayers.

The sign at the Dream Motel inexplicably gleaned that I longed to see Ayers Rock, as did Ernest. Decades ago my young son, inspired by a favored Australian cartoon series that we watched together, drew pictures of it with red crayon inside my notebooks, obscuring the writing beneath. The hopes of one day going with Sam were dashed, but I would make my way surely with his blessing. In the closet my boots were waiting, their soles curiously embedded with the red soil of a place I had never been.

I called Sam a few days later but didn't yet mention the great red monolith. Instead we talked about red horses.

—It was Secretariat's birthday a few days ago.

—Now, how would you know the birthday of a horse? Sam laughed.

—Because it's a horse you love, I said.

—Come to Kentucky. I'll tell you the story of Man o' War, another big red. We can bet on the Derby and watch it on television.

—I will, Sam. I'll take a look at the field before I do.

On May Day, I sat on my porch in Rockaway. There was nothing but blue wildflowers growing in my little patch, as if it had been seeded by sky. Out here, though only a long subway ride away, the worldview falls away. What remains is a smattering of butterflies, two ladybugs and one praying mantis. It is all about my desk with a cabinet portrait of the young Baudelaire and a photo-booth shot of a young Jane Bowles and an ivory Christ without arms and a small framed print of Alice conversing with the Dodo. It's all about a slightly blurred Polaroid of me and Sam at Café 'Ino a few years ago when things were almost normal.

I studied *The Morning Telegraph*, as I had done as a young girl mimicking my father, a meditative handicapper. Maybe it was in my blood, for I was usually pretty good at picking horses, especially to place. I couldn't muster a feel for this particular field, though, but finally settled on Gun Runner. Two days later I bought a ticket to Cincinnati, paid a driver to take me over the state line to a gas station near Midland where I would be picked up. I spotted the white truck approaching. Sam and his sister Roxanne. I noted with a pang that Sam wasn't driving.

Last Thanksgiving, Sam had picked me up at the airport in his truck, with some effort, using his elbows to guide the steering wheel. He did the things he could, and when he couldn't he adjusted. At that time, he was editing *The One Inside*. We'd wake early, work for several hours, then take a break, sitting outside on his Adirondack chairs mostly talking literature. Nabokov and Tabucchi and Bruno Schulz. I slept on the leather couch. The sound of his breathing machine had a soft, enveloping hum. Once he had prepared for bed, pulled up his cover and folded his hands, I knew it was time to sleep and something within me acquiesced.

—Everybody dies, he had said, looking down at the hands that were slowly losing their strength, though I never saw this coming. But I'm alright with it. I've lived my life the way I wanted.

Now, as always, we fell right into work mode. He was in the homestretch, bent on finishing *The One Inside*. Physically, writing had become increasingly tiresome, so I would read the manuscript to him and he'd consider what was needed. His last edits required more thinking than writing, searching for the desired combination of words. As the book unfolded, I was dazzled by the bravado of his language, a narrative mix of cinematic poetry, pictures of the Southwest, surreal dreams and his singular dark humor. Inklings of his present challenges emerged here and there, vague yet undeniable. The title was gleaned from a Bruno Schulz quote, and when the question of a cover came up, it was right there, a photograph by the Mexican photographer Graciela Iturbide that Sam had tucked in the corner of the kitchen window. A Seri woman with loose, dark hair and flowing skirts in the Sonoma desert carrying a boom box. We looked at it over our coffee, nodding complicity. From the window, we could see his horses coming up by the fence. Horses that he could no longer ride. He never said a word about it.

On the morning of the Derby we placed our bets. It was going to be a fast track and none of us had a feel for a winner. Sam told me to box Gun Runner, guaranteeing a payout if it came in third, so I did. The race was set to go off at 6:51 Eastern Daylight Time, the 142nd running at Churchill Downs. As we gathered around the TV, it occurred to me that it was my late father-in-law Dewey Smith's birthday. When my husband was alive we also would gather around the TV at his parents' house to watch the Derby, and I wondered what horse Dewey might have favored. He was born in eastern Kentucky and his father was a sheriff who patrolled his county on horseback, with a notched rifle by his side. Three years in a row to Dewey's astonishment I had picked the horse to come in second, but today my horse Gun Runner came in third.

After dinner, I went out and sat on the front steps to look at the sky. The moon was a waning crescent, like the tattoo between Sam's thumb and forefinger. Some kind of magic, I whispered, more a plea than anything else.

———

A FEW DAYS AFTER I got home I received a small parcel and a note from Sam's sister. Sam had sent his pocketknife along with my winnings, wrapped in newspaper. I placed the knife in a glass cabinet next to my father's coffee cup. In the days that followed I felt tired and uncertain, not my usual way at all. I reasoned I was just at a low point, maybe fighting off a cold, and decided to do nothing.

The thirtieth of May was Joan of Arc's feast day, traditionally a day of enforced optimism. I was still feeling low and my cough escalated, yet I had the impression that something was bubbling underneath, that something was going to happen, like the birth of a poem or a small volcano erupting. That night I had the dream, one that seemed more gift than dream, medicinal and pure like an untainted arctic stream.

In the dream, we were alone in the kitchen and Sam was telling me of the heat in the center of Australia, and the ruby glow of Ayers Rock and how back then—in the day, as he called it—before they had resorts, he went there alone without a guide, by jeep, and saw it for himself. A spool of memory, like a grainy home movie, unwound and we watched as he got out of the jeep and commenced the forbidden climb. He gathered the tears of the Aborigines. They were black, not red, and he slid them into a small, worn leather pouch, like the gris-gris pouch that fell from the pocket of Tom Horn when they hanged him for God knows what.

I looked at Sam sitting motionless in his mechanized wheelchair that was parked before the kitchen table. His head had become a massive diamond slowly turning, emitting rays from crusted eyes. There was still hope then, even as messed up as it was. The room contracted and expanded like a lung or the bellows of a bagpipe. I swiftly followed his orders, disengaging the oxygen.

—Are you ready? he said.

—But how can you possibly breathe?

—I am no longer in need of it, he answered.

We journeyed until Sam found the spot he was looking for, then we sat on wooden crates, just waiting. A woman came and set to work, placing a low wooden table before us. Another brought two bowls but no utensils and a third carried a cauldron of steaming soup. The fetus of a black chicken floated in a broth of eighteen medicinal herbs, with nine yolks, forming a corona about its tiny head. A solar system of yolks, a perfect arc from shoulder to tiny shoulder.

—It's an ancient recipe, he explained, this broth comes from the sun. Drink up, it's a gift. I was handed a ladle and the women withdrew. I was dismayed that I was obliged to be the one to destroy the floating image that had already taken on the aspect of an embroidered holy card.

—You'll have to do it, he said, looking down at his hands.

I was sure it would make me sick, but he winked at me, so I drank, and in an instant a path appeared, a stardust path. We rose but I turned away, feeling confused. Then Sam started talking, he told me the story of Man o' War, the greatest racehorse that ever lived. And he told me it was possible to love a horse as much as a human being.

—I dream of horses, he whispered. I've been dreaming of them all my life.

We traveled on and I did get sick just as I feared. After three days I was still sweating and vomiting. I was drained and dehydrated and we had to stop at every imaginable stream so I could drink. On the fourth day, I saw that Sam was scooping up the water with his own hands.

—How could it be? I was thinking.

—The broth is working, he said, reading my thoughts.

Yet he was not really speaking. He was standing at the edge of an enormous gorge, greater than the Grand Canyon, greater than the diamond crater of Siberia, chewing on the dead end of a piece of straw. I sat very still. He was listening to a lone stampede, as if from the breath of a deadly dream. And then I saw, through his mind's eye, the greatest racehorse that ever lived, a white star on his forehead and his back red and glowing like an ember in the dark.

My father's cup

INTERMISSION

*N*othing *is ever solved. Solving is an illusion. There are moments of spontaneous brightness, when the mind appears emancipated, but that is mere epiphany.*

These were the words kinetically trailing, as if that damn sign had followed me all the way back to New York City. I sat up with a start. I guess I had nodded off briefly at my desk working on my computer, for a redundant train of errant vowels ended an unfinished sentence.

—Needed are proofs. Only proofs grant the mathematician true distinction.

—To say nothing of the poet detective, I reply grumpily.

I rise and go into the bathroom, stopping to wipe the toilet seat as the ghost of a paw print can be detected. Proofs, I muse, washing my hands. Euclid knew it. Gauss and Galileo. Proofs, I say aloud, scanning the space around me. In a moment of decisive action, I open the window, strip the bed and nail the top sheet to the wall, scrutinizing its whiteness. From a carton of old supplies, I unearth a black illustrator pen, the kind artists used in the twentieth century. After standing motionless for several minutes I trace the known bends and curves of the stratosphere on the surface of the sheet.

In the days to come the notations on the sheet multiply. Bits of Greek, algebraic expressions, morphing Möbius strips, and the rusting coil of a spring streaking the sheet with traces of an indecipherable equation.

—Nothing is solved, chides the sign.

—Nothing solved, cries justice and the listing scales.

Following their voices, I enter the library of a great hall with massive volumes containing images tipped and pre-served, as in a scrapbook, with penciled captions. The ship approaching the harbor of Brundisium as Virgil breathed his last. Ghost ships frozen in the arctic sea, hung with veils of ice glistening like African diamonds. Floating bones of prehistoric giants that were once proud icebergs. Migrant vessels overturning and the blue faces of children and col-lapsing hives and a dead giraffe.

Nothing is solved, whispers a curl of dust as I replace the heavy volume on an equally dusty shelf. Not a damn thing, cosmically or comically. I can feel the sign tracking me. In retaliation I track right back, though sorry to see it somewhat enervated, not itself at all.

—Nothing is solved, repeats the sign.

—Nothing solved, echoes nature.

I seek solace in the clouds rapidly changing shape—one fish, one hummingbird, one snorkeling boy, pictures of gone afternoons.

It is the unprecedented heat and the dying reef and the arctic shelf breaking apart that haunts me. It is Sandy slipping in and out of consciousness, battling a run of bacterial infections, while mapping his own apocalyptic scenarios straight from the bowels of the Heart o' the City Hotel. I can hear him thinking, I can hear the walls breathing. Perhaps a break is needed, an intermission of sorts, withdrawing from one scenario, allowing something else to unfold. Something negligible, light and entirely unexpected.

Some time ago during an intermission of *Tristan and Isolde* at La Scala, seeking a bathroom I inadvertently entered an unlocked chamber where costumes of Maria Callas were being prepared for display. There before me was the distinctive black caftan she wore as Medea in the film directed by Pier Paolo Pasolini. There was also her robe, headdress with veil, several strings of weighty amber beads and the heavily embroidered chasuble she was obliged to wear while racing through the desert in heat so intense that Pasolini was said to have directed in swim shorts. His Medea, though played by the world's most expressive soprano, did not sing, which Sandy and I found to be exquisitely irreverent, adding a dissenting tension to her magnificent performance. I lifted the amber and ran my hand down the length of her robe, the same that had transformed her as the witch of Colchis. The warning rang and I hurried back to my seat, my companions sensing nothing unusual whatsoever. They had no idea that in the space of an intermission I had touched the sacred vestments of Medea, whose threads contained the sweat of the great Callas and the invisible handprint of Pasolini.

Nothing is solved, but I'm off anyway, I say, packing my small suitcase. The same drill: six Electric Lady T-shirts, six pair of underwear, six of bee socks, two notebooks, herbal cough remedies, my camera, the last packs of slightly expired Polaroid film and one book, *Collected Poems* of Allen Ginsberg, a nod to his coming birthday. His poetry will accompany me on a short lecture tour, one that will take me to the cities of Warsaw, Lucerne and Zurich, free by day to disappear down side streets, some familiar and some strange, leading me to unexpected discoveries. A bit of passive wandering, a small respite from the clamoring, the cries of the world. The streets where Robert Walser walked. The grave of James Joyce just up a hill. The gray felt suit of Joseph Beuys hanging unattended in an empty gallery in Oslo.

IN MY TRAVELS, I disconnect from the news, reread Allen's poems, an expansive hydrogen jukebox, containing all the nuances of his voice. He would not have disengaged from

the current political atmosphere but would have jumped right in, using his voice in its full capacity, encouraging all to be vigilant, to mobilize, to vote, and if need be, hauled into a paddy wagon, peacefully disobedient.

As I pass from border to border the atmosphere of motion takes on the quality of otherworldliness. Children seem animated, paper dolls in little jackets pulling along their own suitcases adorned with the badges of their own travels. I long to follow them but continue on my way winding down my predestined journey to Lisbon, the city of cobbled night.

It is here I meet with the archivists of the Casa Fernando Pessoa, where I am invited to spend time in the beloved poet's personal library. I am given white gloves, enabling me to examine some of his favorite books. There is detective fiction, collected poems of William Blake and Walt Whitman, and his precious copies of *Flowers of Evil, Illuminations* and the fairy tales of Oscar Wilde. His books seem a more intimate window into Pessoa than his own writing, for he had many personas who wrote under their given names, but it was Pessoa himself who acquired and loved these books. This small realization intrigued me. The writer develops independent characters who live their own life and write under their own names, no less than seventy-five of them, each with a separate hat and coat. So how can we know the true Pessoa? The answer lies in front of us, his own books, an idiosyncratic library perfectly preserved.

Recording the poem *Salutation to Whitman* for the oral archive, written by one such creation—Álvaro de Campos—lifts my spirits. Coincidentally I had read Allen's poem for Whitman the night before, and the librarians who shepherd his books are delighted to hear of the connection. Time swiftly passes and I forget to ask if they have any of Pessoa's wide-brimmed hats, which I assume to be in their original hatboxes, perhaps within a concealed closet along with an array of overcoats once used for his clandestine night walks. Returning to my hotel I pass his likeness, forged in bronze, that nevertheless seems set in motion.

It is in the city of Pessoa that I linger, though I could hardly say what exactly I am doing. Lisbon is a good city to get lost in. Mornings in cafés scribbling in yet another notebook, each blank page offering escape, the pen serving, fluid and constant. I sleep well, dream little, simply exist within an uninterrupted interlude. On a twilight walk a strain of music drifts through the old city, evoking the low, sonorous voice of my father. Yes, *Lisbon Antigua*, a favorite of his. I recall as a child asking him what the title meant. He smiled and said it was a secret.

Brothers and sisters, the evening bells are tolling. Lanterns illuminate the patterned streets. Within an Edward Hopper–like silence, I follow the path that Pessoa once walked, at all hours. A writer of multiple minds, so many

Café A Brasileira, Lisbon

ways of seeing and so many journals, labeled with so many names. Treading the tiled walkways, touching the ivy-covered walls, I pass a window and notice a gentleman standing at the bar, slightly bent, scrawling in a notebook. He wears a brown overcoat and a felt hat. I try to enter but there is no door. I watch him through the glass and the face I see is familiar yet unfamiliar.

—He's just like you and me.

It was the sign back again, my clairvoyant nemesis, but in the center of my enforced solitude, I could not help but be gladdened.

—Do you really think so? I ask.

—I am absolutely sure, it answers, somewhat affectionately.

—You know, I whisper, you were right, I really am going to Ayers Rock.

—The soles of your shoes are already red.

I did not ask the sign how my husband fared in whatever space was allotted to him in the universe. I did not ask the fate of Sandy. Or Sam. Those things are forbidden, as entreating the angels with prayer. I know that very well, one cannot ask for a life, or two lives. One can only warrant the hope of an increasing potency in each man's heart.

The cobbled streets lead me to my provisional home. My room is an enchanting mix of simplicity and uncommon detail. There is a carved wooden bed with a linen coverlet and a small desk with a white lattice paperweight and a

stained ivory letter opener. The meagre supply of statio-
nery, enough for a sole missive, is nonetheless of a finely
burnished parchment. The bathroom floor is a gleaming
mosaic pieced with tiny blue and white tiles like the base
of a Roman bath.

I sit at the desk and remove my old Polaroid Land
camera from my sack to inspect the bellows. The book of
Allen's poems is opened to *A Supermarket in California*. I
picture him cross-legged on the floor next to his record
player singing along with Ma Rainey. Expounding on
Milton and Blake and the lyrics of *Eleanor Rigby*. Bathing
the forehead of my young son, suffering a migraine. Allen
chanting, dancing, howling. Allen in his death sleep with a
portrait of Walt Whitman hanging above and his life com-
panion, Peter Orlofsky, kneeling by his side, covering him
in a swathe of white petals.

I am tired but content, believing I have somewhat unraveled the city's secret. In the drawer of the nightstand is an
illustrated pocket map, a little guide to the town of Sabrosa,
the birthplace of Magellan. I have a vague memory of
drawing a ship circling the world at the kitchen table. My
father making a pot of coffee, whistling *Lisbon Antigua*. I
can almost hear the notes melding with the sound of the
percolator. Sabrosa, I whisper. Someone is fastening my
seat belt. The wooden bed in the corner of the room seems
so far away, and all is but an intermission, of small and
tender consequence.

HOME IS THE SAILOR

The sheet I had tacked to my wall was still there, hanging like a limp sail. I had completely forgotten about it. The state of mind that induced the intricate markings had shifted. What's more, heavy rains had caused the skylight to leak and the sheet was now stained with rust-colored streaks that seemed to contain a language of their own that drifted in and out of my sporadic sleep.

No moon, black sky above. Get a grip, it's only 4 a.m., I tell myself as I plod into the bathroom, strangely spacious, as if two small rooms had been gutted to produce one unnecessary anomaly. There is an old farm sink, a small tiled shower, an obsolete claw-foot tub overflowing with linens and enough room to throw down a mat and stretch out on hot summer nights. Perched against the wall is a slightly mottled mirror with a faded postcard of *Victoria,* the second smallest of Magellan's ships, manned by the explorer himself.

Sensing no sleep on the horizon, I roll out the mat and resort to an old game, originally designed to trick myself to sleep. I imagine myself a sailor in the time of the great whaling ships on a lengthy voyage. We are in the center of a violent storm and the captain's inexperienced son catches his foot in a length of rope and is pulled overboard. Unflinching, the sailor leaps into the storm-tossed seas after him. The men throw down massive lengths of rope and the lad is brought to the deck in the arms of the sailor and carried below.

The sailor is summoned to the quarterdeck and led to the captain's inner sanctum. Wet and shivering, he eyes his surroundings with wonder. The captain, in a rare show of emotion, embraces him. You saved my son's life, he says. Tell me how I can best serve you. The sailor, embarrassed, asks for a full measure of rum for each of the men. Done, says the captain, but what of you? After some hesitation the sailor answers, I have slept on galley floors, bunks and hammocks since a lad, it has been a long time since I have slept in a proper bed.

The captain, moved by the sailor's humility, offers his own bed, then retires to the room of his son. The sailor stands before the captain's empty bed. It has down pillows and a light coverlet. There is a massive leather trunk at its

He eyes his surroundings with wonder

foot. He crosses himself, blows out the candles and succumbs to a rare and wholly enveloping sleep.

This is the game I sometimes play when sleep is elusive, one that evolved from reading Melville, that takes me from the mat on the bathroom floor to my own bed, affording grateful slumber. But it was not to be on this markedly humid night. The mischievous monkey, toying with the climate, toying with the coming election, toying with the mind, producing sour sleep or no sleep at all. Punctuating my tangled musings, the rain suddenly beats down on the skylight. I watch the red streaks break apart and realign, an indecipherable Sumerian text. There is a bucket in the closet, which I place beneath the leak, anticipating intermittent dripping, a bucoloic rhythm of its own.

I turn on my small television, careful to avoid the news. On the screen, a blond Aurore Clément is whispering in French as she packs the bowl of an opium pipe.

—There are two of you, she says, drawing closer to Martin Sheen, one who kills and one who doesn't.

—There are two of you, she repeats, slipping out of the frame. One walks in the world, one walks in dream.

She rises, drops her robe and slowly unties the panels of mosquito netting framing their bed. He draws from the pipe, watching the outlines of her body moving behind the pale netting. She unhurriedly unties each panel as he reaches for her, through the fog of cinematic war.

At last I feel sleep closing in, saying good night to the

sailor and Captain Willard and the French girl with the opium pipe. I can hear my mother reciting a poem by Robert Louis Stevenson. *Home is the sailor, home from the sea. And the hunter home from the hill.* I can see her hand pushing a roller, repainting a bedroom or smoothing out new wallpaper. The credits are rolling, it says *Apocalypse Now Redux*. The net closes around me, the rubber band is cut and blood rushes in a vial, drawing one unfinished thought.

For Sandy

IMITATION OF A DREAM

Sandy open your eyes. I traced these words on the window with my left hand, over and over, as if producing a spell. An ardent Artaud type of spell, one that would actually work. But no mystical effort could realign the directive of the Reaper. It was July 26. The prelude ended, Parsifal knelt before the mortally wounded swan and Sandy Pearlman left the earth.

On that same day, there was news of wildfires in Southern California, the dense smoke reaching all the way to Nevada. The Democratic Convention was blazing with its own fiery mix of hope and desperation. *Solar Impulse 2*, the solar-powered aircraft, made its last leg around the world. The gods Sandy had celebrated buried their marble heads in sand-colored towels. He would never enter the Matrix with his beloved Keanu Reeves, or circulate in the mad world of Donnie Darko or listen to *Angel of the Morning* or eat devil's food cake. Sandy, with the thinking heart, composing a vast reinterpretation of history through an ongoing dream, was now seeking his kingdom of Imaginos, captain of his own charmed ship.

The days of summer stretched. Sunflowers bloomed in every field. In my solitude, I imagined wolves crying. I followed them, trudging the icy perimeter, passing a gingerbread house, an entire village trapped on an ice sheet as big as the smallest of the thirteen colonies. A colony adrift. I looked up at the sun, as if drawn by a child's hand, with each ray distinct.

On the fifth of August, his birthday, the birthday of my son, I opened the top of my desk and found the last package Sandy had sent me, one that had arrived during my travels and was tucked away unopened. He would often surprise me, for no particular reason, with gifts of Aztec chocolate, tins of sockeye salmon from Seattle, Solti's traversal of the four operas of *The Ring of the Nibelung*. I packed it with some things, got a half pound of chestnut pasta and some green onions and took the long subway ride to my little bungalow in Rockaway Beach. I struggled with the combination lock on the battered cyclone gate, as dried salt had jammed the numbers. The yard was a battleground of towering ribwort and trampled Queen Anne's lace.

Once inside, I flung open the windows. I hadn't come to Rockaway in several weeks and the house needed a bit of airing. I shook sand out of my Chinese rug and vacuumed and mopped the red-tiled floor with oolong tea. I wanted coffee, but dampness had crystalized what was left in my jar of Nescafé.

Opening the small package, I pictured Sandy hastily addressing it, securing it with an excessive amount of scotch tape. It was a CD of *Grayfolded*, an experimental Grateful Dead recording, difficult to find and much coveted. He had promised me that he would find it and he did. Happy Birthday, Sandy, I said aloud, thank you for the present. I felt extremely calm, even lighthearted. I rinsed off the dishes, prepared myself some spaghetti and sat on my porch with my plate in my lap, staring at my yard where persistent finger grasses had overrun the herbs and wildflowers, like settlers on the Indian plain.

I sat motionless, did not rise, or gather my tools, or hack or weed. I suddenly felt dead—no, not dead, more otherworldly, a grateful kind of dead. I could feel life scurrying about, a plane overhead, the sea just beyond and the unfolding notes of *Dark Star* drifting through the grid of my screen door. I could not bring myself to move, and let myself be transported elsewhere, long before I knew Sandy, long before I listened to Wagner, to another summer at the Electric Circus, where a young girl slow-danced with an equally young boy, awkwardly in love.

BLACK BUTTERFLIES

Last days of August with Sam in Kentucky. We had been working for most of the afternoon. I went out back around twilight for a short break and was drawn to strange movements on the stone ledge surrounding the garden. It was covered with black butterflies, scores of them, one on top of another, in a fluttering frenzy in the half-light. There was a faint whistling sound, their mortal song perhaps, dark wings their mourning coats. A photograph I had taken of my grown children at their grandfather Dewey's funeral came to mind. My son in a black Stetson hat and my daughter in a black dress.

Sam looks up and grins when I reenter; we immediately return to work. An early revision of a recent manuscript. There are several changes and new passages which he verbalizes to avoid the struggle of writing by hand. Some time ago he told me that one must write in absolute solitude, but necessity has shifted his process. Sam adjusts and seems invigorated by the prospect of focusing on something new.

His sister Roxanne makes me tea. You're coughing, she says. Sam smiles. She's had that darn cough for forty-five years. Sam sits stoically in his wheelchair, his hands resting on the table. His old Gibson rests in a corner, a guitar he can no longer play. And the reality of the present hits hard, no banging on the typewriter keys, no roping cattle, no more struggling with his cowboy boots. Still I say nothing of these things and neither does Sam. He fills in the silences with the written word, seeking a perfection he alone can dictate.

We continue, me reading and transcribing, Sam writing out loud in real time. The deeper task is to rescue aloneness. The aloneness required to write, the absolute necessity to claim those hours as though hurled through space, like the astronaut in *2001*, never dying, just continuing on and on in the realm of film that never ceases, into the infinitesimal, where the Incredible Shrinking Man is still shrinking, and in that universe, is its perpetual lord.

—We've become a Beckett play, Sam says good-naturedly.

I imagine us rooted in our place at the kitchen table, each of us dwelling in a barrel with a tin lid, we wake up and poke out our heads and sit before our coffee and peanut-butter toast waiting until the sun rises, plotting as if we are alone, not alone together but each alone, not disturbing the aura of the other's aloneness.

—Yep, a Beckett play, he repeats.

As night falls, his sister prepares his needs. I settle into my makeshift bed, situated where I can see him.

—Are you all right? he says.

—Yes, I'm good, I answer.

—Good night, Patti Lee.

—Good night, Sam.

I lie there listening to the sound of his breathing. There are no curtains and I can see the silhouettes of the trees. Moonlight illuminates the fragile webs in the corners of the room and the edge of his bed and the low coffee table between us laden with books and my feet poking out from the quilt that covers me. The portrait of night I see through the window beckons. Unable to sleep I get up and go outside to breathe the air, looking up at the stars and listening to the crickets and the bullfrogs in full throttle. I use the flashlight on my phone and return to the garden of the house. The black butterflies are still there, motionless, covering a portion of the ledge of the garden wall, but I can't really tell if they are dead or just sleeping.

The writer's shoes

AMULETS

I sat in the center of my own disorder. The boxes stacked against the wall contained two decades of Polaroid images. Remembering a promised mission, I set about the task of sorting through countless numbers of them, mostly shots of statues and altars and defunct hotels. I spent hours but had no luck locating the photograph I had promised Ernest—the games of Roberto Bolaño. I felt a twinge of regret, but in the end I hadn't the slightest notion of where to send it if I did. *Going in circles. Going in circles.* Lyrics to a song, though I couldn't remember which one. *Going in circles,* surrounded by images of cities and streets and mountains I could no longer identify, like small evidences of a crime long gone cold.

I separated some of the photographs I had taken in the last year or so. The back wall of On the Bridge covered with *Wolf Girl* posters. The coffee place whose letters were

disproportionate to the actual interior. An unmade bed, a bad angle of Ernest's truck. A pelican perched atop the WOW Café sign. An action shot of a charm bracelet sliding off the dashboard of a Lexus; the many charms of Cammy. Each one tells a story she had said.

Cammy and Ernest and Jesús and the blonde, all characters in an alternative reality, black-and-white cutouts in a Technicolor world. Even the sign and the security guards on the beach. A world that in itself was nothing, yet seemed to contain an answer for every unutterable question in early winter's impossible play.

Piling the Polaroids back into a box, I found several glassine envelopes in a manila folder. There were various shots of the Guggenheim in Bilbao and the fifties-style lobby of the beach hotel in Blanes. Images that I had obviously favored and set apart. The writer's shoes. The tomb of Virgil. Two linden trees in the mist. One after another, each a talisman on a necklace of continuous travels. And behind a picture of a small girl with dark curly hair was Bolaño's games. Not really much of anything, just a closet interior, but exactly what I had been looking for.

I sat on the floor somewhat satisfied, not a fruitless search at all. I gazed at the photograph of the smiling little girl, the daughter of Roberto Bolaño. She had not played with his games, but had games of her own. I pictured several such girls, turning in circles, singing in different languages that somehow seemed the same. Suddenly I was tired. I remained where I was and leaned against the bed attempting to untangle my excessively knotted hair. A brief memory of untangling two gold chains came to mind. Twin golden circles and faces like dangling charms, some close up, some indistinct.

The Unicorn in Captivity, Cloisters

IN SEARCH OF IMAGINOS

Imaginos approached the sun singing songs
nobody knew and stories left undone

—SANDY PEARLMAN

I walked the length of Atlantic Avenue, where I had once bought henna and reggae records that you couldn't find anywhere else. I stopped to rummage through some over-flowing trunks of discarded costumes in front of an abandoned theater, sequined robes and bangled skirts glinting in the Indian summer sun. I unearthed a fragile silk dress, cut wide yet weightless, as if spun by a factory of militant spiders. I left my jacket atop a box and slipped the dress over my T-shirt and dungarees. I kept digging and found a coat, also lightweight and somewhat frayed. It was my kind of coat, entirely without seams, riddled with small holes at the hem and sleeves. There was a rubber band in the right pocket, caught in some thread. I pulled my hair up in a ponytail and walked up the metal ramp and took my seat on the *Jefferson Airplane*. The plane, not the band, but when I looked out I realized I was in a van, not a plane, which was thoroughly confusing. The driver turned on the radio, a baseball game interrupted by radio calls in another language, somewhat musical, maybe Albanian. He took a different route than I requested and ignored any questions. He kept grunting and scratching his thick arms and I noticed flakes of skin falling on the black leatherette armrest. We were gridlocked on a bridge, only it was not a usual bridge and seemed to be slightly swaying. I was more than tempted to get out and cross on foot.

And so it continued. No matter which way I stepped or whatever plane I was on, it was still the Year of the Monkey. I was still moving within an atmosphere of artificial brightness with corrosive edges, the hyperreality of a polarizing pre-election mudslide, an avalanche of toxicity infiltrating every outpost. I wiped the shit from my shoes again and again, still going about my business, that of being alive, the best I could. Although an insidious insomnia was slowly claiming my nights, giving way to the replaying of the afflictions of the world at dawn. At some point I tried sleeping with the television on, a small one stationed on the right side of my bed. Avoiding the news, I accessed the on-demand channel, choosing random episodes of *Mr. Robot* to play at low volume. I found the monotone voice-over of the hoodied hacker Elliot quite soothing and lay in limbo, which was almost like sleeping.

IN EARLY OCTOBER, Lenny and I flew to San Francisco for Sandy's memorial. I felt a wave of irrational bitterness. It should have been in Ashland, I thought, with the entire *Ring* cycle performed ground-level, without sets, on a circular stage, where the mourners could keep shifting position every hour, experiencing the *Ring* from every angle. Sandy left a hole, and with his unexpected departure, his devotion to Wagner, Arthur Lee, Jim Morrison, Benjamin Britten, *Coriolanus, The Matrix* and a revolutionary vision of a Medea meant to unhinge then reframe the theatrical world. With no family to speak of, one by one friends spoke fondly, if not humorously, of his youth in Stony Brook, his contributions to music technology, his songs and visionary production of the Blue Öyster Cult. He was noted as a revered lecturer at McGill University, specializing in the obscure convergence of classical composition and heavy metal.

Roni Hoffman and her husband, Robert Duncan, Sandy's lifelong guardian angels, had selflessly negotiated his complicated and ultimately failed convalescence; they both spoke poignantly of decades of friendship. The glowing threads of their reminiscences interlaced with my own and I found myself on a long-ago drive with Sandy to the Cloisters. He still had his sports car then and wanted to show me the majestic tapestries called *The Hunt of the Unicorn,* canonical works created in the sixteenth century by unknown hands on behalf of unknown royalty. The hangings were massive, at least twelve-foot-high pictorial scenes of intricately interwoven wool warp and silk, metallic threads, silver and gilt wefts.

Sandy and I stood before *The Unicorn in Captivity.* The mythic animal was encircled by a wooden fence surrounded by a carpet of wildflowers, vibrantly undead. Sandy, an admirable weaver of words, mapped out the terrible events that led to its capture, beguiled then felled by maiden betrayal.

—The unicorn, Sandy said solemnly, is a metaphor for the terrible power of love.

On its knees, the unicorn shimmered in its distress. I had seen and admired it solely in books, not comprehending its magnitude, its innate power to arouse a buried belief in the existence of a mythical creature.

—This unicorn, he continued, is as alive as you and me.

Lenny tapped me gently on the shoulder and led me to the small stage. We performed *Pale Blue Eyes,* then a slow ritualistic version of *Eight Miles High,* both meaningful to Sandy. Lenny played electric guitar with his eyes closed. I could not help but feel distraughtly distant, like Nico performing her elegy to Lenny Bruce.

Lastly, Albert Bouchard, the charismatic drummer

from Blue Öyster Cult, embarking on Sandy's master-piece, *Astronomy*, armed solely with an acoustic guitar—a feat requiring a high degree of selflessness, considering the august scope of the piece. Years ago, I had watched with Sandy, both transported, as the Blue Öyster Cult per-formed the same song with Albert at the helm in an arena for eighteen thousand people. Albert, now alone, delivered *Astronomy* with a pathos that broke all stoic barriers, and all wept.

Lenny and I went back out into the night and walked through Chinatown. We passed the same wise-monkey bench as I had on my own. We walked forever, it seemed, up and down the streets of San Francisco, stopping for a breath at the corner of Fillmore and Fell. I was wear-ing the clothes I had found in the overturned trunks on Atlantic Avenue. Lenny was wearing a black jacket that had belonged to my husband with black jeans and a black leather vest. I lifted my hem to tie my bootlace.

—Nice dress, he said.

The band joined us two days later at the Fillmore to honor Sandy. As I got out of the car, two fellows approached me. They looked nothing alike but gave the impression they were the same person. The one with a shaved head gave me a necklace. I put it in my jacket pocket without looking at it and once again climbed the metal steps to the stage door, imagining Jerry Garcia doing the same. Lenny was already there to greet me, opening the heavy iron door. I froze for a moment before reaching him, suddenly conscious of the repetition of our every action.

That night, performing *Land of a Thousand Dances*, I closed my eyes during the breakdown, improvising all the way to the Baltic, to the land of Medea. I walked that barren stretch, following Medea's sandaled feet, as she had followed Jason. The golden fleece shimmered, blinding all who dared to glance upon it. I saw the flame in Medea's transparent heart and felt the blood boiling in her veins. A high priestess yet also a country girl, she was unable to match wits with Jason's people. Forced to draw from her primal self she dresses as a fox to obscure the hunt. Her small sons sleep. Jason's sons. She loved him and he betrayed her. I watched as she raised her white arm encircled with heavy bracelets. I saw the fleece lose its luster. I saw the dagger find their small hearts.

The band played loudly, the people were rowdy, spontaneously erupting. Perhaps some followed the thread wound from the fleece of Jason to the fleecing of Medea and the terrible witchcraft of the beyond, but it didn't matter. I sang for Sandy, and the poetry that spewed was for him. I beheld his flashing smile, those ice-blue eyes, and felt for a moment that joyful arrogance that spread its mantle on the altar of opera, mythology and rock 'n' roll. I was exactly where he was, and we stood, each sensing the other, on the precipice of irredeemable tragedy.

WHY BELINDA CARLISLE MATTERS

The hotel phone would not stop ringing. It was the front desk, but which front desk, which city, which month? Okay, it was October, Seattle, in a spacious room with a view of a massive air-conditioning unit, and I was slated to deliver a talk on the importance of libraries. It was four in the afternoon and I had fallen asleep in my coat. The dress I wore to the memorial was draped across the couch. I had arrived and dropped my stuff and just passed out. Somewhat groggy, I washed my face and prepared for my talk, mentally collating a succession of libraries I had frequented since a child, when a library card gave entrance to entire series of books: *The Bobbsey Twins, Uncle Wiggily and His Friends, Freddy the Detective,* all the *Oz* books and Nancy Drew mysteries. Library memories cross-wired with images of my own books, hundreds of books, lying on the bed, lining the right side of a staircase, stacked on the card table in the kitchen and higher stacks on the floor, against the wall.

Once in the lobby, I was pounced upon and spirited away, much like Holly Martins in *The Third Man,* when he was herded from his hotel in Vienna to deliver a talk about the role of the existential cowboy in American literature. Like Holly I felt excessively unprepared. Standing before a full house, I figured better to take the personal route and spoke of the importance of a library to a nine-year-old bookworm living in a rural community in southern New Jersey, a place devoid of culture, not a single bookstore, though thankfully a small library, roughly two miles from our home.

I spoke of how much books have always meant to me and how every Saturday I would go to the library and choose my books for the week. One late-autumn morning, despite menacing clouds, I bundled up and walked as always, past the peach orchards, the pig farm and the skating rink to the fork in the road that led to our sole library. The sight of so many books never failed to excite me, rows and rows of books with multicolored spines. I'd spent an inordinate amount of time choosing my stack of books that day, with the sky growing more ominous. At first, I wasn't worried as I had long legs and was a pretty fast walker, but then it became apparent that there was no way I was going to beat the impending storm. It grew colder, the winds picked up, followed by heavy rains, then pelting hail. I slid the books under my coat to protect them, I had a long way to go; I stepped in puddles and could feel the icy water permeate my ankle socks. When I finally reached home my mother shook her head with sympathetic exasperation, prepared a hot bath and made me go to bed. I came down with bronchitis and missed several days of school. But it had been worth it, for I had my books, among them *The Tik-Tok Man of Oz*, *Half Magic* and *A Dog of Flanders*. Wonderful books that I read over and over, only accessible to me through our library. As I recounted this little tale I noticed a few people in the audience with handkerchiefs, recognizing something of that book-struck young girl in themselves.

Early the next morning, I got up and had coffee at a place called Ruby's. I remembered eating here with Lenny and Sandy a few years ago after a concert at the Moore Theatre, the oldest in Seattle, notorious for its Egyptian décor. The great Nijinsky and Anna Pavlova had danced on its stage, and the likes of Sarah Bernhardt, the Marx Brothers, Ethel Barrymore and Harry Houdini played their best hands here as well. It was once segregated, and people of color were relegated to the high balcony seats. This stain upon the theater was not without irony, as those same seats were rewarded with the best acoustics. That was the year Sandy and I drove to Ashland to see *Coriolanus* at the Oregon Shakespeare Festival. Or as Sandy put it, to witness the fall of a condition of hubris that Shakespeare had raised to the realm of the mystical. I finished my breakfast and walked over to deliver a donation to the Bread of Life Mission. A homeless fellow in a long, gray overcoat and purple watch cap was scrawling a message on a brick wall with a thick piece of pink chalk. I slipped a five in his cup next to a makeshift bed of flattened cardboard, then watched his fingers as the words slowly emerged: *Belinda Carlisle Matters.*

—Why? I asked. Why does Belinda Carlisle matter?

He stared at me for a fairly long time that extended into an even longer time, all the way back to when cities were merely hills. He shifted his gaze from me to over his shoulder, then down to his shoes, then finally looked up and answered in a low voice.

—She's got the beat.

This was a true Sandy moment. Had he been here he would have surely declared this a momentous truth. I merely smiled and shrugged. I didn't doubt him but I didn't put much stock in it, either, until several days later, back in New York City, unable to sleep, I was scrolling the channels and stopped at some music infomercial. I think it was one of those deals where they sell twenty-two CDs from the eighties, or maybe it was just girl groups, but there on the TV were the Go-Go's, doing *We Got the Beat* on some English pop music show. All the girls were cool, but it was Belinda who had the moves, nothing flashy, kind of *Beach Blanket Bingo* with a modern swing and a bit of French

Paradis, leggings and little high heels. Yeah, Belinda, I said aloud, you got the beat.

Her exuberance was infectious. I imagined a nonviolent hubris spreading across the land, like the boys in *West Side Story* buoyed by a mounting swagger, singing *When you're a Jet* . . . Hundreds of thousands of girls and boys flooding the open perimeters, taking on Belinda Carlisle's moves, singing *We got the beat*. And soldiers laying down their arms and sailors leaving their posts and thieves the scenes of their crimes and all at once we're in the epicenter of one grand musical. No power, no race, no religion, no apologies. And with this vast spectacle racing through my head, some part of me leapt up and sashayed down the road, entering the scene, joining the chorus increasing ad infinitum, like William Blake's angels streaming from the turning pages of the book of life.

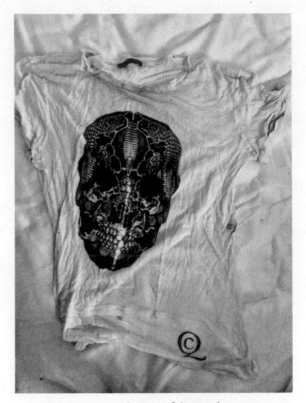

It was the Day of the Dead

THE HOLY SEE

It was the Day of the Dead. The side streets were dressed in sugar skulls and a kind of stale madness hung in the air. I had bad feelings about an election in the Year of the Monkey. Don't worry, everyone said, the majority rules. Not so, I retaliated, the silent rule and it will be decided by them, those who do not vote. And who can blame them, when it's all a pack of lies, a tainted election lined in waste? Millions poured down a hole lined with plasma, spent on endless contentious television commercials. A true darkening of days. All of the resources that could be used to scrape away lead from the walls of crumbling schools, to shelter the homeless, or to clean a foul river. Instead, one candidate desperately shovels money down a pit, and the other builds empty edifices in his own name, another kind of immoral waste. Nonetheless, despite all misgivings, I voted.

Election night I joined a gathering of good comrades

and we watched the terrible soap opera called the American election unfold on a large-screen TV. One by one each stumbled off into dawn. The bully bellowed. Silence ruled. Twenty-four percent of the population had elected the worst of ourselves to represent the other seventy-six percent. All hail our American apathy, all hail the twisted wisdom of the Electoral College.

Unable to sleep, I walked over to Hell's Kitchen. A few bars were already open, or else they never closed, and no one swept up or cleared the booths readying for a new day. Maybe as to deny it was a new day or merely to curtail its unfolding. It's still yesterday, the debris called out, there's still a chance in hell. I ordered a shot of vodka and a glass of water. I had to pick the ice out of both my drinks, dumping it into a dish of stale pretzels. The radio was on, a real one, Billie Holiday singing *Strange Fruit*. Her voice, one of laconic suffering, produced shudders of admiration and shame. I pictured her sitting at the bar, a gardenia in her hair and a Chihuahua in her lap. I pictured her sleeping in a rumpled white skirt and blouse on a diesel-fueled tour bus, turned away from a white Southern hotel despite the fact that she was Billie Holiday, despite the fact that she was simply a human being.

The overhead fan was covered in dust. I watched it turn, or rather the motion of its turning. I must have momentarily nodded, catching the wisp of the end of another passing song. *New York, I love you, but you're bringing me down.* Pine-covered hills, morning eggs in a basket.

—Another drink?

—I'm not much of a drinker, I was saying. Just some black coffee.

—Do you want milk?

The waitress was pretty but had a piece of skin hanging from her lip. I couldn't stop staring at it. In my mind, it got bigger and heavier, then detached and plopped into an imagined bowl of steaming broth that widened, forming a bubbling pool, where an imitation of life emerged. I shook my head. The things that transport us can be so random. It was definitely time to get moving, but an hour later I was still there. I wasn't hungry or thirsty but I thought that maybe I should order something to justify sitting at the same spot for over an hour, but no one seemed to care, perhaps the same postelection paralysis claiming us all.

The days passed, and what was done could not be undone. Thanksgiving gone and Christmas Eve looming, I meandered through the shopping streets to the beat of an internal whisper: *Don't get me anything. Don't get me anything.* Guilt wetted the dried particles of defeat; how did it come to such a bad end? Another case of imbalanced social outcry. Silent, silent night. Assault rifles wrapped in foil stacked beneath artificial trees decorated with tiny golden calves, targets set up in the backs of snow-covered yards.

Dead of winter yet there seemed to be no temperature at all. Crossing Houston Street, I noticed that the infant Jesus was absent from the Nativity scene in front of St. Anthony's. There were no birds perched on the shoulders of St. Francis. Plaster maidens with white headdresses were preparing an empty feast. I was never so hungry, never so old. I plodded up the stairs to my room reciting to myself, *Once I was seven, soon I will be seventy*. I was truly tired. *Once I was seven*, I repeated, sitting on the edge of the bed, still in my coat.

Our quiet rage gives us wings, the possibility to negotiate the gears winding backwards, uniting all time. We repair a watch, optimizing an innate ability to reverse, say, all the way back to the fourteenth century, marked by the appearance of Giotto's sheep. Renaissance bells ring out, as a procession of mourners follow the casket containing the body of Raphael, then sound again as the last tap of a chisel reveals the milky body of Christ.

All go where they go, just as I went where I went, finding myself in a shadowed corner reeking of whole egg and linseed oil in the workshop of the brothers Van Eyck. There I saw a ripple of water executed in such an exacting fashion as to induce thirst. I witnessed the precision of the younger as he touched the sable ends of his brush to the wet wound of the Mystic Lamb. I hurried away lest we collide and continued on rapidly toward the unfolding twentieth century, soaring past the green fields of rural prosperity dotted with crosses commemorating the slaughtered sons of the Great War. These were not ungraspable dreams but a frenzy of living hours. And in these fluid hours I witnessed wondrous things until, tiring, I circled above a small street lined with old brick houses, choosing the roof of the one with a dusty skylight. The hatch was unlocked. I removed my cap, shaking out some marble dust. I'm sorry, I said, looking up at a handful of stars, time is running and not a single rabbit can keep up with it. I'm sorry, I repeated, descending the ladder, conscious of where I had been.

December 30th. I sailed past my seventieth birthday into the year ending, ankle deep in confetti. I whispered *Happy New Year* to my well-traveled boots, just as I had done exactly one year ago. One year to the day having pulled into the Dream Motel, where certain things were rendered uncertain and a sign predicted I'd be going to Uluru. One year to the day when Sandy Pearlman was still alive. One year to the day when Sam was still able to make a cup of coffee, and write with his own hand.

Without a trace of hyperbole

THE MYSTIC LAMB

Traveling with an almost religious simplicity to a place I had never heard of, a town near Santa Ana, back west, where Sam was staying for the winter. A town, he said, where it would not stop raining. Come, he commanded softly, and just like that I packed a rain jacket, flannel shirt, some socks and a small but profusely illustrated book on the *Ghent Altarpiece*. On the plane, I tried not to think about the state of things, of anything unpleasant. There was a bit of turbulence, which was all right with me, just disruptive weather patterns harboring no personal intentions. I opened the small book and concentrated on the great altarpiece, a long-favored preoccupation.

The magnificent polyptych was painted on oak in the fifteenth century by the Flemish brothers Hubert and Jan van Eyck. The whole of the altarpiece was committed with such supple eloquence that it was venerated by all who beheld it and believed by many to be a conduit to the Holy Spirit. Just as the archangels had been divine instruments, a physical embodiment of a phone call from God. The Virgin Mary received such a call, depicted on the exterior panel of the Annunciation, the announcement of the Incarnation by the angel Gabriel; one could only imagine the burning network of fear and exaltation that emanated from this single transmission. The Virgin kneels within a kaleidoscopic void ornamented with her words inverted in burnished gold. Not a garish leaf but a Flemish leaf, applied by incomparable Flemish hands. Once I touched the surface of the exterior panel and was filled with awe, not in the religious sense, but for the artists who realized it, sensing their turbulent spirits and their majestic concentrative calm.

Mary is pictured again in a more serene manner above the central panel of the interior, where she takes her place on the left of God the Son. Words span the double halo curving about her slightly bowed head, declaring her the unblemished mirror of Divine Majesty. Despite all accolades she exhibits a wholesome simplicity, the sweetened nature worthy of the Queen of Sorrows.

Beneath is the crux of the altarpiece, the *Adoration of the Mystic Lamb,* said in its time to have induced swooning. A sacred mystery made visible through a work of art. The triumphant yet stoic lamb, accepting all earthly suffering, stands upon the altar as blood from his side pours into the

Grail, in accordance with prophecy. Thirst will cease to be thirst and wounds will cease to be wounds, though not in the way that's expected.

What will happen to us, I wondered, closing the book. Us being America, us being humanity in general. The look in that lamb's eyes seemed unremitting, but is it possible that the blood of benevolence may not be infinite and will one day cease to flow? I imagined the withering spring, the drying of the Samaritan well, a disturbing convergence of stars.

I felt a dull throbbing in my temple. I noted my sleeve was stained from grazing the palette of the painter whose brush stroked the dark wound of the lamb. Had that really happened? I couldn't recall a face, but I know I had wept, though without the salt of tears. I remember standing there only a handful of days ago, dumbfounded until cruelly spun from the time of *The Adoration* into the realm of the now. The stain, I reckoned, looking out at the western sky, was at least as real as memory.

—What is real anyway? Sam had asked not long ago. Is time real? Are these dead hands more real than the hands in dreams that can cast a line or turn a steering wheel? Who knows what is real, who knows?

In San Francisco I boarded a shuttle to Santa Ana. Sam's sister Roxanne picked me up at the airport. Her sunny disposition was a welcome respite, for the sky was nothing but gray and it was raining, just like Sam said. We pulled up

in front of a white clapboard house. I walked up the steps and saw Sam through the screened door before he saw me. He looked more like Samuel Beckett than ever, and I still harbored the hope that I would not be destined to grow old without him.

We worked in the small kitchen. I slept on the couch. I could hear the incessant rain beating against the awning protecting the porch. We were a world away from Kentucky, Sam's land and horses. Away from everything his. Our days centered on his manuscript, destined to be his last, an unsentimental love letter to life. Every once in a while, our eyes would meet. No masks, no distances, only the present, the work being the principal thing and we its servant. In the evenings, it was tabled and all cheerfully submitted to the ritual of hoisting down the wheelchair, negotiating porch steps and taking a walk into town to the café that served Mexican hot chocolate. I walked slightly behind in the mild drizzle, experiencing a dizzying sense of bygone days hanging on to Sam's arm as we tripped down Greenwich Village streets.

The silence surrounding the little house was unnerving. There was nobody around when we took our nocturnal walks. I hated myself for feeling restless. Sam felt it too but understood; he was born restless. When I had to leave California, it was still raining. I got in the car with Roxanne. We pulled away from the white clapboard house, the ivy-covered trellis and the oversized watering can. I promised her I'd keep in touch. *Thirst will cease to be thirst and wounds will cease to be wounds.* As we approached the Santa Ana airport, I glanced at my phone. There was no message from the angels, not a call, not a single ring.

We are the living thorns

THE GOLDEN COCKEREL

The night before the Inauguration there was a waning crescent. I tried to ignore the tightness in my throat, a mounting sense of dread. I wished I could sleep until it was over, a Rip Van Winkle kind of sleep. In the morning, I went to the Korean spa on Thirty-Second Street and sat in their infrared sauna for nearly an hour. I sat there coughing with a small mound of sticky tissues and thought of Hermann Broch mapping out *The Death of Virgil* in his head while confined in prison. I thought of Virgil's tomb in Naples and how he wasn't actually there because his ashes were lost in mysterious circumstances in the Middle Ages. I thought of Thomas Paine's words: *These are the times that try men's souls.* Outside, the rain ceased but high winds remained. And what was truth remained the truth. It was the last day of the Year of the Monkey and the golden cockerel was crowing, for the insufferable yellow-haired confidence man had been sworn in, with a Bible no less, and Moses and Jesus and Buddha and Mohammed seemed somewhere else entirely.

The following night gongs sounded and dragons spewing paper flames rolled down the streets of Chinatown like enormous pull toys. It was the 28th of January. The cock of the new year had arrived, a hideous thing with puffed chest and feathers the color of the sun. *Too late too late too late,* he crowed. The Year of the Monkey was over, and the fire rooster, waiting in the wings, made a grandiose entrance. I skipped the lunar year parade though I watched the fireworks from my stoop. It occurred to me that I had grazed the sidelines of both the East and West Coast celebrations, the alpha and omega of the Year of the Monkey, yet had not participated in either. Perhaps not so surprising, other than proximity, for even as a child I found it difficult to surrender wholeheartedly to such festivities, actually dreading the drone of the annual Thanksgiving parade with its floats and marching bands or the manic excitement of the Mummers parade. Inwardly I always felt completely lost in swirls of revelers, like Baptiste unwillingly swept into the throes of the manic carnival at the end of *Children of Paradise.*

Nonetheless I found myself in Chinatown a few days later, in a trusted pharmacy, consulting an old Chinese herbalist who had made me healing teas in the past. The body is a reactive center, he told me, reflecting on my symptoms and general malaise. All these afflictions are reactions to outer stimuli, chemicals, the weather, food intake. It's all a question of balance, the system is just recalibrating. Eventually all will disappear, whether a rash or a cough. One must remain serene, and not indulge these reactions with too much energy. He gave me three packets of tea. One was golden, one was red and another the color of sage. Pocketing them, I reentered the cold, noticing the signs of celebration mostly gone, some remnants of paper lanterns, bits of confetti, a discarded plastic monkey on a broken stick.

I walked to the end of Mott Street and descended the stairs of Wo Hop to meet Lenny for congee. In the seventies, a bowl of duck congee cost ninety cents. Wo Hop has always been open, boisterous, serving congee until 4 a.m. All of us ate there back then, often in the early hours after the new year, many of us broke, many who are dead. Lenny and I ate our congee and drank oolong tea in silent gratitude, still alive; born three days apart, seventy and silver haired, bowing to fate. We didn't talk about the Inauguration, but it hung heavy in the atmosphere, as anxious hearts merged with anxious hearts.

That night I drank the golden tea and did not cough in my sleep. I dreamed of a long train of migrants walking from one end of the earth to another, far beyond the ruins of what had once been home. They walked through deserts and barren plains and strangling wetlands where wide ribbons of inedible algae, brighter than the Persian sky, wrapped around their ankles. They walked dragging their banners behind, clothed in the fabric of lamentations, seeking the extended hand of humankind, shelter where none was offered. They walked where wealth was shuttered within works of architectural mastery, immense boulders encasing modern huts ingeniously obscured by dense indigenous vegetation. The air within was dry, yet all doors, windows and wells were hermetically sealed as if in anticipation of their coming. And I dreamed that all their hardships were viewed on global screens, personal tablets and two-way wristwatches, becoming a popular form of reality-based entertainment. All watched dispassionately as they tread unforgiving ground, hope bleeding into hopelessness. Yet all sighed with emotion as art flourished. Musicians rose from their torpor composing mesmerizing works of symphonic suffering. Sculpture sprang as if from the covered ground. Muscular dancers depicted the torments of the exiled, rushing the length of great stages as if overcome by nomadic futility. All watched, riveted, even as the world in its dependable folly kept spinning. And I dreamed the monkey leapt upon it, this mirrorball of confusion, and broke into dancing. And in my dream it was pouring, as if with a heartbroken vengeance, yet unconscious of the weather I went out without a raincoat, walking all the way to Times Square. People were gathering before a mammoth screen watching the Inauguration and a young lad, the very same who had alerted the populace that the emperor had no clothes, cried: Look! He's back again, you let him out of the bag! The festivities were followed by a new installment of a reenactment of the trials of the migrants. Wooden boats streaked in gold lay abandoned in the shallow waters. A gilded mascot descended, screeching and flapping its monstrous wings. Dancers writhed in agony as barbs of compassion pricked their feet. The onlookers wrung their hands in sympathetic fury, yet this was nothing to those walking the earth, the circumference killers, tracing words in the windswept sand. Portray us if you must, but we are the living thorns, the pierced and the piercing. And I awoke and what was done was done. The human chain was in motion and their voices played in the air like a cloud of ravaging insects. One cannot approximate truth, add nor take away, for there is no one on earth like the true shepherd and there is nothing in heaven like the suffering of real life.

I tried to call you, he said

A NIGHT ON THE MOON

It was a third-rate café bar. That is to say it had a degree of anonymity that concurrently camouflaged and exposed any questionable goings-on. No place to hide within its colorless walls, but on the other hand, few would come across it, an anonymous-looking joint on a side street just off the boards. Hard-luck joes, bookies and stoolies, the last vestiges of an era only a dirty cop might recognize.

I scanned the layout as I entered. Same scattered tables, yellow-flecked linoleum floor, a few booths. I had been here before, some two decades ago, back when they served the best ham and eggs with real Virginia ham. The pool table was gone but otherwise the same somber deal, absent of décor, unless you wanted to count the mountain-scenes calendar. A place where minding your own business was a minor religion.

The fellow closest to the door was hunched over, staring

into his cup as if deciphering a dark prophecy emanating from its grains. Next to him an ashtray full of stubs, the perfect still life. Two guys in the back were talking low and so close their heads touched across the table.

I stood by the bar, waiting to be served. There was a faded photograph of Manolete the bullfighter in a gilded wooden frame with silk rosebuds glued to the corners. I wanted coffee but was compelled to order a drink. I downed a shot of vodka, wondering how I fit in with this woebegone bunch. Maybe like a drifter, not well-heeled but not down, either, maybe somebody who missed the boat or at least some shining opportunity.

—What kind of vodka is this?

—Who wants to know?

—Well, it's watered down, but it's damn good vodka.

The bartender feigned being hurt.

—Kauffman's. It's Russian stuff.

—Kauffman's, I repeated, then wrote it down on a small flip-top notebook I had in my back pocket.

—Yeah, but you can't get it here.

—But it's here, I said.

—Yeah, but you can't get it here.

I just sighed. Was it all a dream? Was everything a dream? Beginning with the Dream Motel straight on through all the monkey-induced mischief. I was in the middle of this circular rumination when I sensed that I was not alone. Making a quick scan of the bar, I spotted him. I hadn't noticed him when I came in, but he was there all right, sitting in semi-darkness at a corner table tossing folded bits from his wallet. He hadn't crossed my mind in quite a while, not so much since he left me stranded in a landscape near-biblical in its emptiness. I was determined to catch his eye but he looked straight through me. *We met at the WOW,* I was saying in my head. *Well, actually we never met. I just sat down at the table and wandered into the conversation, the one about 2666, the one covering the dog races in St. Petersburg.* Ernest did nothing to indicate he was getting the message, so I walked over and sat down. He began talking as if picking up in the middle of a former conversation, something about the opening scene of *Apocalypse Now.*

—Martin Sheen drunk out of his mind, an act of pure bravery, the bravest thing on film, baffling that they pulled it off. The broken mirror and all that blood. Not movie blood. Martin Sheen blood.

Then he stood up and headed to the john. I went up to the bar and got another drink. I'm not much of a drinker, but I figured diluted vodka, good vodka at that, wouldn't hurt, not even in the dead of the afternoon. I motioned to where Ernest had been sitting.

—Do you know what he's been drinking?

—Who wants to know? he said. But he placed an obscure-looking bottle of tequila before me. I asked him to wait a few minutes, then bring the bottle over and offer him a drink on the house. I laid some money down, when a woman came in with a wig case and some dry cleaning. She went through a door behind the bar. The guys with their heads a few inches apart had not moved. In fact, no one moved, no one reacted to her, or to me. Two women invading a third-rate man's world.

I went back to Ernest's table. We sat awhile in edgy silence.

—I wonder how Joseph Conrad would like *Apocalypse Now,* I said, mostly to break the ice.

—That's a rumor, he said. There's no truth in it at all.

—No truth in what?

—That it's just a redo of *Heart of Darkness.*

—Well, yeah, that's not true at all, but it did inspire it. Even Coppola said that. That's half its beauty, how Coppola transformed a classic into a modern classic.

—A twentieth-century classic, not even modern anymore.

He suddenly leaned toward me.

—Who had the darkest heart? Brando or Sheen?

—Sheen, I said without hesitation.

—Why?

—He still wanted to live.

The bartender brought the bottle over and set a shot glass before Ernest. Pour yourself one, on the house, he said. Ernest filled it to the brim. They water this stuff down, he told me, finishing it off rather quickly.

—Everything comes from the heart. The drunken heart. You ever been drunk? Really drunk? I mean drunk for days, lost in the romance of everything down, pitched in the swirl of absurdity.

That's what he said, pouring himself another tequila. It occurred to me that I had never seen him drink anything but coffee. Of course, I knew little about him. His last name, for instance. But it's like that sometimes. You know an imperfect stranger like no one else. No last names, no birthdates, no country of origin. Only eyes. Strange tics. Small indications of a state of mind.

—He'll build that damn wall, he was saying, and the money will come from the pockets of the poor. Things are changing at a speed we never dreamed. We'll be talking nuclear war. Pesticides will be a food group. No songbirds, no wildflowers. Nothing but collapsing hives and lines of the rich getting ready to board a ship for a night on the moon.

Then he went quiet. We both did. Ernest looked tired, the ravages of life seemed more pronounced than just a year ago. I could feel the bitter sadness that seemed to permeate the room. It rose like a suffocating gas, and the few scattered patrons looked up as if they heard a child crying.

—I'm here about Tangier Island, he mumbled.

I stood up, wrote *Tangier Island* in my notebook and slipped it into my back pocket. Ernest nodded slightly but gave no indication that I should stay. I noticed a penny on the floor and bent down to pick it up. As I exited I had the feeling that if I reentered, even if only a moment later, everything would be altered. Suddenly Technicolor, with the new bartender in charge, in her wig, full makeup, dry-cleaned dress.

I walked out and sat on a nearby bench. I wondered what Ernest was doing in Virginia Beach. The little I knew of him pointed to some kind of mission. But then again, he may be wondering the same thing of me. I had come on an impulse, pure nostalgia. A bus to Richmond just to look at the James River where I had once stood with my brother Todd talking about Edgar Allan Poe and Roberto Clemente, his favorite ballplayer. Todd looked like Paul Newman. The same ice-blue eyes. The same self-effacing confidence. You could count on him for anything. Anything except staying alive.

A few more stragglers, a guy walking his dog, an old Chinese woman wearing wooden sandals with thick socks with her grandson holding an oversized red ball. The red of the ball seemed to solarize. A big ball of silvery blood. The kid had a thin jacket on but didn't seem cold; the wind was more prominent over the water, dying down on the boards.

I wondered if I was waiting for Ernest to come out, though in all likelihood he was already gone. He seemed beaten down. Not the same agitated force he had been when we met at the WOW. Something went down and something drew him here. Some other conspiracy, maybe,

something to do with Tangier Island. I saw him stagger
from the bar. I had the urge to tail him as he headed down
the boardwalk, but it seemed too dramatic. I watched him
for a few minutes, then, distracted by a swooping gull,
missed the moment when and where he turned off. The
opportunity gone, I thought about looking around for a
room. I had a lot of cash on me, credit card, notebook and
a toothbrush. In the distance, a kid on a bike approached
my bench and dismounted.

—Excuse me, he said. A guy named Ernest said to give
you this. He handed me a brown paper lunch bag.

I looked up and smiled. Where is he now? I said.

—I don't know, he just asked me to give you that.

—Thanks, I said, fishing in my pocket for a dollar.

I had a few questions to ask but he jumped back on his
bike and kept going. I watched him growing smaller and
smaller, receding into the horizon, like one of Magellan's
ships. Sighing, I opened the sack and pulled out a beat-up
paperback, the English translation of *The Part About the
Critics*, obsessively notated in Spanish. I flipped through
the pages to the dreams of water, where the pinup blonde,
the Liz Norton of the lot of us, had referenced a space
break. Reading it made me restless for a city. An unforgiving city. Low-rise housing. Mexico City in 1949. Miami in
1980. I could feel the insidious fingers of memory rustling
through the underbrush like the dismembered hand of the
pianist scrabbling toward Peter Lorre's throat in *The Beast*

with Five Fingers. One of my brother Todd's favorite movies, the thought of which triggered unscripted scenes, other pictures of life. Todd smiling in the sun on the plot of land where he would build a house for his wife and daughter. Todd leaning over a pool table with a cigarette dangling. Driving across Pennsylvania in a truck with no heat and small clouds forming as we sang along to oldies on the radio. *My Hero. Butterfly. I Sold My Heart to the Junkman.* Not now, I said, shaking it off, and reopened the book and began at the beginning. The critics seemed more alive than the passersby and suddenly the sea was no longer the sea, but a backdrop for words, some of the greatest sequences of words strung together in the twenty-first century.

When I looked up time had flown, as if on its own tiny plane. Ernest was standing only a few feet away. He seemed in total command of himself, not a bit intoxicated. I walked toward him, somewhat relieved yet hardly willing to go back in circles with him.

—I'm just a writer, I said wearily, nothing more.

—I'm just a Mexican who believes in truth.

I stared him down. He squirmed a bit, then laughed.

—OK. My father was Russian, but he didn't live long.

—Was your father named Ernest?

—No, but he was.

I smiled even as I felt a surge of melancholy. A flash of a wallet, a hand extracting a photograph of a woman in a dark flowered dress with a boy in short pants, his hair neatly combed. Ernest's eyes registered that he knew what I was seeing.

—Why Tangier Island? I finally asked.

—Since it suffered Hurricane Ernesto the island is receding into the sea. I have to make amends.

I noticed clouds moving in. Rain, I was thinking.

—You see, there's a saying carved in Old English on a wooden plank on one of the oldest structures built in America. *This is Tangier Island. As it goes, so do we.*

—Have you actually seen it? I asked.

—You don't see things like that. You feel them, as in all important things; they arrive, they come into your dreams. For instance, he added slyly, you're dreaming now.

I whirled around. We were standing in front of that same third-rate café.

—See, he said in a voice oddly reminiscent of some other voice.

—You're the Dream Motel sign, I suddenly blurted.

—It's the Dream Inn, he said, fading.

A KIND OF EPILOGUE

First Muhammed Ali died, then Sandy and Castro and Princess Leia and her mother. A lot of rough things happened, begetting things even more terrible, and then there was the future that came and went, and here we are still watching the same human movie, a long chain of deprivation playing out in real time on massive perpetual screens. Heart-wrenching injustices constituting the new facts of life. The Year of the Monkey. The death of the last white rhinoceros. The ravaging of Puerto Rico. The massacre of schoolchildren. The disparaging words and actions against our immigrants. The orphaned Gaza Strip. And what of existence only a reach away? What of the stoic writer who held a miniature of the world in the palm of his tattooed hand? What will happen to him? I had asked myself, shuttling back and forth to Kentucky. When I first wrote these words, I didn't yet know, and one could fast-forward or move backwards but time has a way of still going, ticking away, new things one cannot alter, cannot get down fast enough. We used to laugh, me and Sam, about this disconnect: you write in time then time is gone and in trying to catch up you're writing a whole other book, like Pollock losing contact with a painting and making a whole other painting and losing the thread of both and in a rage kicking through glass walls. I can tell you this, the last time I saw Sam, his manuscript was all but done. It was there on the kitchen table like a small monolith, containing the uncontainable, a bright flicker that could not be extinguished. Why birds? wrote Sam. Why birds? echoed his sister. Their song wafted from a boom box partially buried in the sand. Why birds? cried the old man. And they flapped their wings, found then broke formation and eventually disappeared. What would happen to the writer? The answer is now encased in an epilogue that wasn't meant to be an epilogue but has turned into one since all one can do is try to keep up as Hermes races before us with his chiseled ankles. How do we lay this out, other than speak the truth? Sam Shepard would not physically climb the steps of a Mayan pyramid or ascend the arched back of a sacred mountain. Instead he would skillfully slide into the great sleep, just as the children of the dead city spread waxed-paper sheets over mounds of corpses rushing toward paradise. You get there faster sliding downhill on waxed paper, every child knows that. This is what I know. Sam is dead. My brother is dead. My mother is dead. My father is dead. My husband is dead. My cat is dead. And my dog who was dead in 1957 is still dead. Yet still I keep thinking that something wonderful is about to happen. Maybe tomorrow. A tomorrow following a whole succession of tomorrows. But getting back to the moment, which is already gone, I was alone in Virginia Beach, suddenly left holding the bag. The brown paper bag containing the worn copy of *The Part About the Critics*. I stood there attempting to absorb the absurd truth of the punch line uttered by Ernest. Come on, you, I said to the mirror, one that had fallen from a compact with the gilt peeling away, one easily conjured. Come on, I said to one eye and then to the wandering other, get focused. You got to get a grip on the whole picture. The mirror slipped from my hand and as it hit the ground I could hear the voice of Sandy saying *shards of love, Patti, shards of love*. And then I walked in the other direction, the longer stretch of boardwalk. No one knows what is going to happen, I was thinking, not really. But then again, what if one could telescope the future? What if there, on the boardwalk, was a view finder that projected all the way through 2017 into the following Year of the Dog? What manner of things would one see? What spectacular and terrible twists of the golden rope, unraveling here and there, from the alpha to the omega? A few notches, a few million notches. The death of the writer the transfiguration of a friend the flecked eyes of Jesus Christ the flames engulfing Southern California the collapse of the Silverdome and men falling like chess pieces carved from the weight of centuries of indiscretions and the slaughter of worshippers and the guns and the guns and the guns and the guns. And there, on a winter's afternoon, there on the map where the three great faiths once moved through the marketplace in kind, where David conquered, where Jesus walked, where Mohammed ascended. Look in shame as pilgrims are shooed away, troops made ready and who knows when the first stone will be thrown. The neutral capital slated to be the new capitalist stronghold. Shall the olive wither? Shall the mountains shudder? Will the children of the future never taste the sweetness of brotherhood? I kept walking, it seemed as if the boardwalk had no beginning or end. I knew there had to be a brass telescope mounted somewhere on the boards and I was determined to find it, not exactly a telescope but an instrument of *beyondness,* right on the esplanade. The kind you put a quarter in to see the islands just out of reach, ones occupied by wild horses—say, Cumberland Island or even Tangier Island. My pockets were brimming with coins so I set up camp and concentrated, first on a freighter, then on a star, and then all the way back to Earth. I could actually see that ball the world. I was in space and could see it all, as if the god of science let me peer through his personal lens. The turning Earth was slowly revealed in high definition. I could see every vein that was also a river. I could see the wavering illness air, the cold deep of the sea and the great bleached reef of Queensland and calcified manta rays sinking and lifeless organisms floating and the movement of wild ponies racing through the marshes overrunning the islands off the Georgian coast and the remains of stal-

lions in the boneyards of North Dakota and a fleet of deer
the color of saffron and the great dunes of Lake Michigan
with sacred Indian names. I saw the center which was not
holding and, just as Ernest had described, a small island
like the navel of an orange gasping for breath and one huge
tortoise and one darting fox and several old muskets rusting in the high grass. There were old men climbing the
rocks and lying in the sun with their hands folded. There
were small boys stomping the wildflowers. And I saw the
ancient days. There were bells tolling and wreaths tossed
and women turning in circles and there were bees performing their life-cycle dance and there were great winds and
swollen moons and pyramids crumbling and coyotes crying and the waves mounting and it all smelled like the end
and the beginning of freedom. And I saw my friends who
were gone and my husband and my brother. I saw those
counted as true fathers ascend the distant hills and I saw
my mother with the children she had lost, whole again.
And I saw myself with Sam in his kitchen in Kentucky and
we were talking about writing. In the end, he was saying,
everything is fodder for a story, which means, I guess, that
we're all fodder. I was sitting on a straight-back wooden
chair. He was standing looking down at me just as always.
Papa Was a Rolling Stone was playing on the radio, which
was brown tweed, sort of forties-looking. And I thought,
as he reached down to brush the hair from my eyes, the
trouble with dreaming is that we eventually wake up.

EPILOGUE OF AN EPILOGUE

I implore you all. Temper fear with reason, panic with patience, and uncertainty with education.

—ABDU SHARKAWY

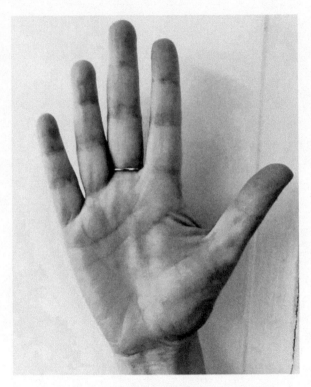

It's in our hands

The Year of the Monkey has long past, and we have entered a new decade, one that has so far played out with mounting challenges and a systemic nausea, though not necessarily induced by illness or motion. More of a psychic nausea that we are obliged to work off in every way available. Though harboring hopeful dispatches, the new year has unfolded with our personal and global concerns eclipsed by a profound lack of judgment.

We greet 2020 as our constitutional moral center is being redesigned in an increasingly immoral way, governed by those professing to have a hold on Christian values yet sidestepping the core of Christianity—to love one another. Their necks turn from the suffering as they willingly follow one lacking an authentic responsiveness to a waning human condition. I had hoped for a more enlightened scenario for our new decade, imagining ceremonial panels opening, as the wings of great altarpieces on feast days, revealing 2020 as the year of perfect vision. Perhaps these expectations were naïve and yet were truly felt, just as the anguish of inequity is felt, a dark blot that will not go away.

Where is brightness? Where is prudent justice? we ask, standing our ground with mental plow, burdened with the task to stay balanced in these unbalanced times.

He was a full metal rat

A PANEL FOR THE YEAR OF THE RAT

THERE IS A SAYING in the canons of lunar astrology that the Monkey needs the Rat. I'm not sure in what capacity, though some say that Rats are able to cheer Monkeys up when they're feeling down, for when together the air is filled with laughter. Of course, we are speaking not only of the species themselves but also of certain inherent qualities of those born in the year of either augury. In any event, we are, at this very moment, entering the lunar Year of the Metal Rat, to be vastly celebrated in our great cities, especially those containing magnificent Chinatowns, with massive displays of fireworks, sacred lion dances, and confetti and multicolored tinsel floating from the sky. Festivities to be capped with a parade on February 10, as the full snow moon rises, with floats and dragons and effigies of the year's namesake. In an abstract gesture of solidarity, I dig into a box of old records and unearth Frank Zappa's *Hot Rats*. The girl on the cover, rising from a deserted swimming pool, is Miss Christine, the fragile Victorian beauty of Girls Together Outrageously, known as the GTOs.

Hot Rats came out at the end of 1969. At the time, I was living with Robert Mapplethorpe at the Chelsea Hotel, and we often talked with her in the lobby. She was an ethereal being, with a mane even wilder than mine and skin like peach fuzz. Somewhere in early 1970, Miss Christine

Miss Christine rising, shot by Andee Eye

petitioned me to join her revolutionary band, and though it wasn't the right vocation for me, I was flattered. Shaking her slender hand, I had the impression I was facing a delicate bird of prey. That was over half a century ago, which is hard to fathom, for I can still picture her wide-eyed and soft-spoken, head cocked, a pirate's fair daughter who never saw twenty-three. With a nod to Zappa's young protégée, I slip the record from the sleeve and examine it carefully, discovering it covered with tiny scratches, like the claw prints of a circling band of rats.

A turntable spins straight back through time. I place the album jacket on my desk, temporarily obscuring a small Tenniel print of Alice conversing with the Dodo. Propped next to that is a birthday gift from a dear friend, an upright crystal rat washed in gold that I have christened Ratty. He will preside over my room as my lunar talisman. For that's how it works; we look to the rising Metal Rat with unguarded optimism, for each new year begins with its designated lunar creature, with its particular armor and distinctive personality, and the integral belief that things will soon be better.

FESTIVITY PANEL

Things will soon be better. That is what I wrote some days ago in anticipation of worldwide celebration, the atmosphere already charged with readiness for the new. The Metal Rat is the first sign in the twelve-animal cycle of the Chinese zodiac, absolutely a time of optimistic renewal. But regrettably an unforeseen twist, a sudden threat of a global pandemic framed the Metal Rat's entrance, dampening spirits, definitely raining on the parade. With China on the verge of a shutdown, I wondered how our own streets were faring and went with Lenny Kaye to Chinatown with hopes to glimpse remnants of the opening celebration, with its traditional glittering debris and perhaps colorful rats on a stick embellished with red-and-gold streamers, to say nothing of a general sense of joy. Those were our child-like expectations. Anticipating crowded streets, we had doubts about finding a parking spot, but amazingly there were plenty. We sat in the Silk Route Café and had a pot of brown rice tea, then took a stroll looking for signs of action.

Though early evening, the streets were eerily deserted, just a few passersby. The restaurants, save for our beloved Wo Hop, appeared to be empty, and we were hard-pressed to find any signs of the first round of festivities. I supposed we were just too late for one party and too early for another.

On the edge of Mott Street there were straggly remains of multicolored tinsel and small clumps of confetti. Where were the trailing vapors of golden dragons of flammable paper bursting into wisps of wishes that when caught in a precise angle of light, certainly come true? In China, things looked bleak for revelers preparing for the year's greatest party. In one swift operation, Beijing canceled large-scale events and temple fairs as the deadly coronavirus insidiously spread. So much for the heralding of the poor Metal Rat, caught in quarantine along with several million people. A virus hysteria mounts as the disease jumps ship from Wuhan to neighboring ports, resulting in travel bans and closed borders. A protective mask lay curled in the gutter by our parking spot. In an effort to thwart contagion, many are wearing such masks. Some wear two, one on top of another. "I have drawn a rat on mine," cries a defiant citizen. "And though we are deprived of our lunar unity, I will celebrate on my own with sparklers in the night." For despite decrees forbidding festivities, the people find a way to externalize their joyous traditions. Stamping their feet with a Bruegel-like fervor, they hold to the certainty that the world will not cease turning, and the lunar new year shall always be, as long as there is a moon; reigning, receding, returning.

St. Nicholas Church

A PANEL UNTO HIMSELF

OKAY, THINGS HAVE GONE AWRY, so how shall one forge on and despite poor tidings connect with the Metal Rat and celebrate? This is the contradictory course of contemplative walking the beleaguered city streets. On the smallest Village streets there is construction everywhere, a relentless restructuring, community gardens excavated in preparation for modern annexes, debris and dumpsters everywhere. All of this disruption is driving our rats from their subterranean homes. In truth, rats, though somewhat hidden, have always been here, but lately due to the heartless demolition of whole cherished blocks, we are certainly in need of the Pied Piper. On a night walk, up and down the streets of scaffolding, they can be seen in nocturnal packs, ripping bags of trash to shreds, strewing remains of our excessive waste across our paths, and attracting their less aggressive brothers and sisters. All this rat preoccupation incites me to look into William Burroughs's *Exterminator!* But I soon realize the protagonist is not on the trail of rats but massive Kafka-like insects.

That same night I dreamed that William appeared from behind a worn velvet curtain and said to me intently, "Look into this Denton thing." I had no sense at all what he was referring to but nodded and walked out of my dream into breakfast. There are mysteries to solve, and there are mysteries that solve themselves. And in some cases, the punch line is delivered as we sleep, though dreams can be tricky, filled with interesting but misleading distractions, roads that are not roads.

Circling this mental maze, I noticed the calendar said February 5. William's birthday. I decided to read something of his, rooting out an inscribed galley of *Queer*. I went to a neighborhood café, ordered a coffee, and reread the introduction, a moving piece of confessional literature. I paused at the part where William revealed that it was the accidental shooting of his wife, Joan, that made him a writer. Reading it segued into an overkill of memories; I suddenly felt the pang of separation, missing his supportive warmth, even from great distances.

William suddenly detoured, speaking of the spiritual connection he felt with the writer Denton Welch when he was writing the novel *The Place of Dead Roads*. This stopped me in my tracks. *Look into the Denton thing,* he had said. I immediately searched to find out if Welch was a real person, which indeed he was, an English novelist born in Shanghai who died in 1948 at the age of thirty-three, coincidentally on my second birthday. I had a feeling that William was not merely giving me a suggested reading list in the perimeters of a dream. It was surely something else. William had channeled Denton while writing and infused his energy into his own work in a way only he knew. We had many discussions about this kind of connection and the phantasmagorical landscape we move through daily but don't mention out loud. I would like to think William was reminding me that we are never alone. Just as Denton was with William, someone out there is with me, spurring me on toward a network of possibilities in the guise of thousands of small unifying electrical currents. "It's right under your nose," he is saying in his low, gravelly voice. "Change the cylinder."

"Yes, William," I whisper, imagining a metal vest, light as tissue, providing a bit of moral armor. It is after all the Year of the Rat, a cunning survivor, and as we cautiously project the fate of the coming year, we must don the best of the resilient rat's qualities, maintaining the enthusiasm to be productive, the courage to face our adversaries, and the will to set things right.

His humanoid face

THE VARNISHED GLOBAL EXIT PANEL

ONCE AGAIN, I awake before dawn, perhaps sensing the waxing snow moon. But there is no snow, only endless rain, and though technically night, there is no night; the sky is murky, and it seems as if the moon has dropped, pressing its milky surface against the four dusty glass panels of my skylight. I feel an oppressive sadness, get up, throw on a jacket, and walk to the corner. The rats scatter, an alarm moans in the distance, and a single passing car. February temperatures rise and fall like the temperament of the twin queens in the chessboard world of Wonderland. Unseasonably warm rain confuses insects and birds. There are no cafés open at this hour. I return to my room somewhat clouded myself. The rain beats against the skylight. April showers in February. The moon is full but not visible, fused in a dense system of night clouds. The cat is crying. She wants to eat, though it is only 5 a.m. I go back to sleep wondering why no less than a thousand sparrows descended from the surrounding trees and gathered in a field where a friend lingered with his dog. The birds swarmed, then touched down all around them, unperturbed by his presence or the incessant barking of the dog. I half drifted into another landscape, finding myself in a massive field of windmills. The modern metal ones that seem related to the sleekly beautiful, much-maligned Concord. I walked through muck and wetlands to get closer and finally was able to touch the base of one, where I felt great relief, much like I did in Uluru when I pressed my hand against the red skin of Ayers Rock. Yet all the while I was thinking I had to be somewhere, that I was late and had to keep moving.

There was an article in the Sunday paper about an exhibition, Jan van Eyck: An Optical Revolution, centering on the small existing body of his work, with important panels of the *Ghent Altarpiece* and nearly one hundred corresponding masterworks from the late Middle Ages. For a brief time, the newly restored *Adoration of the Mystic Lamb,* the centerpiece of the altar, could be viewed in its present room at St. Bavo's Cathedral. I held my breath. W. H. James Weal's massive volume *Hubert and Jan van Eyck: Their Life and Work* sits on my worktable. It is pure detective literature, noting every small evidence of the working existence of the elusive brothers. I have thought of them so much that I once found myself within their realm and so close at hand that I returned to my own with a small smear of paint on my sleeve. This form of mental teleportation was another subject quite dear to William and *Third Mind* partner Brion Gysin, and we often speculated on its endless possibilities.

Suddenly, it seems that the *Mystic Lamb* has entered the public consciousness. All nine panels of the restored altarpiece will reunite in spring, imprisoned for reasons of conservation behind a wall of glass in a new sector of the cathedral. I feel an envious affinity with the restorers, with their scalpels and micromagnifiers, experiencing intimate contact with the artist's handiwork. I wonder, if so absorbed in their work, they also found themselves transported to the studio of the artists, privy to their process, even on hand to witness the entrance of a blessed sheep for the Van Eycks to observe firsthand.

It is the countenance of said sheep that has most captured the attention of the public, for in the scraping away of centuries of overpainting, the restorers have bared its true face. Imagine the astonishment in removing the last filmy veil of discolored varnish to reveal an entirely new face staring back, one decidedly humanoid. In a moment of ecstatic desperation, I am seized with the desire to view it for myself. Looking at the calendar, I find that in spite of many obligations, I do have a five-day window, enough time to make the journey. Regrettably, I cannot be beamed into Ghent as Captain Picard beaming to the surface of Vashti, but I can proceed lightning fast. I trade all my frequent flyer miles for a ticket to Brussels, pack lightly, arrange for the cat to be fed, and set up a driver to get me to Ghent. Just like that, though momentarily affected with an independent trembling, I am off again.

Everything one could ask for

THE PANEL OF SMALL EVIDENCES

MY SMALL SUITCASE was swabbed at security for a random check. As it seems I'm consistently chosen at random, I refrained from sarcasm, maintaining a sense of humor, certain it was the armor of the Metal Rat to my rescue. On the other side of the ocean, my driver was waiting for me when I deplaned. He spoke perfect English, seamlessly describing his many trades, including being the founder of a small sweets company specializing in gummy candies.

—Not bears but cars, he says proudly, something entirely new. Try one, he insists, handing me a packet of tiny jewel-colored gummy cars in the shape of a Volkswagen Beetle.

—Belgium is an interesting country, I say, as we speed toward Ghent. It seems to harbor many secrets.

—And yet we have no government, he answers wryly. Our democracy is being pushed aside.

Thinking of the dismantling of our own, I fall into silence. I smooth my invisible armor, vowing that for a few days nothing will break this traveler's heart. Valentine's Day in Ghent. A three-day destination mission immersing myself in everything Van Eyck, hopefully dissolving the restless fatigue I have found myself battling as of late. We depart before my hotel, situated less than a kilometer from St. Bavo's, where the *Mystic Lamb* dwells.

The breakfast room is bright and friendly. I have a black coffee, small white sausages, plums, and brown bread. Then after consulting a hand-drawn map, I head out.

Crossing the bridge, I stop before the Archangel Michael, perched high above like a warrior weathervane. I stood at the same spot a decade ago with my sister Linda, gazing at the panorama of cathedrals as she, beguiled by the light, took pictures of the water. She had accompanied me to Ghent while I worked with the filmmaker Jem Cohen. In between duties, we hurried off to see the altarpiece but entered St. Bavo's just as it was closing. I remember it was too dark to see the *Mystic Lamb*, but there were a few small bulbs lighting the exterior panels. I walked around the altarpiece and touched the heavy oak frame. As my sister stood guard, I shot a Polaroid in the meager light of the panel depicting the young Mary of the Annunciation. I hastily slipped the forbidden Polaroid into my pocket, exiting somewhat transformed, like a small-time criminal with an illustrious secret.

The strong connection I felt in that brief encounter was not a religious one, more a physical sense of the artist. I felt the aura of his concentration and the sharp gaze of his prismatic eyes. I vowed to one day return, but I never did. Instead, I immersed myself in books, one dark Polaroid, and the realm of memory, existing in the cells, calling to centuries past and occasionally answered. Back in Ghent, I did not race to my most desired destination but proceeded slowly to get a sense of the steps that would take me there.

IN ST. NICHOLAS CHURCH, life-size saints lined the walk-way to the main alter. Each held a symbol of his vocation or fate: a key, a book, a mathematical instrument, and even a golden saw. I sat in a pew several feet from the statue of St. Bartholomew brandishing a strangely modern kitchen knife. Light poured through the high stained-glass windows; I felt a warm rush of well-being and wrote straight through the morning.

Children raced through the pathways laid with Roman stone, streamers tied to their waists that were carried by the wind, flowing behind with the long multicolored tails of kites. Human kites, I was thinking, as they ascended the skies, ignoring their mother's cries. Toward a bracing fog, the color of roses and the pink of the girls' cheeks, disappearing into its benevolent night, and truly they were gone. As Roland's Bell tolled and tolled but none dressed for battle but wept, for no weapon, no amount of force could abate the ravages of plague. No one could stop the burning cards from burning, and the cathedral was overflowing, and many believers laid upon the tiled floor on their bellies with arms outstretched. And all the pieces fell about me like snow. Pieces of a fallen game that no one wins, save time, that keeps flowing at such a pace that I am hurled into an altered present. One fearing a pandemic and the burgeoning scent of global war. A game, all a game, that if nature loses, she will also win, for there is the water of life that is good, and there is the lick of flame that is nothing but light gone awry.

Saying a prayer, I lit a candle for the children we love and those we shall never know. In leaving, I discovered a small piece of sculpture hidden in a niche behind the intricately carved pulpit. An exquisitely cast hand of an artist holding a quill with a nib, perhaps poised to sketch yet also evoking the act of writing. I thought of William's hands and felt a tender sense of connection.

In Ghent, my step was lighter, pen more fluid, and my traveler heart alert to the many chambers of the world. *I am Roland*, the bells tolled. It began to drizzle, so I hurried down the cobbled street back to the hotel. It struck me that these same stones were tread upon by centuries of believers and tradesmen and the children I had envisioned as I sat and wrote in the cathedral. All afternoon it rained heavily, and I was sleepy. I had a shot of Russian Kauffman Vodka and a small meal and retired early with the television on. *CSI: Miami* was dubbed in Flemish, having the same drowsy effect as counting sheep leaping over fences of mist.

On Saturday morning the sun was shining. I had an appointment for a private viewing of the *Adoration of the Mystic Lamb* at St. Bavo's on Sunday evening but decided to see it first with the gathered crowd. All silently filled the small area where the altarpiece was housed. Centuries of darkened varnish and overpainting had been stripped away with the precision of surgeons, revealing distant trees and golden spires. We noted the choir of angels, the adoring populace, the glowing folds of the robes of the kneeling virgins, and the bloodred robe of John the Baptist. The original colors applied in oils bloomed with the intensity of spring, with wildflowers liberally dotting the green fields. Upon a riser stood the stoic lamb, the symbol of sacrifice, his blood pouring into the chalice of the covenant. Above, the Holy Spirit, in the form of a dove, shed rays of love upon the multitude.

The Van Eyck brothers, side by side

On Sunday morning, dark weather loomed, the violent tail of the storms that were pounding the United Kingdom. I made my way from Ramen Street to St. Michael's Bridge, then passed St. Nicholas Cathedral, the ancient Belfry Street, and the rare-coin shop, imagining them jingling in the pockets of fifteenth-century travelers. Turning right across the tram tracks, I located a small park crowned with the monument of Hubert and Jan van Eyck. Overhead, a high crane towered as construction seemingly followed me all the way from New York City. Although the park was closed, I could see the brothers through the cyclone fencing. Hubert with book in hand, Jan with palette greeted by the townspeople with laurels in gratitude for creating a masterpiece magnifying the town's significance, from their medieval moment to the ribboning future.

The winds began to pick up along with a threat of rain. I circled the entire cathedral, exploring niches where renovation was being carried out. An artist who creates masks with bits of found metal came to mind, and there at my feet was a piece of metal scrollwork that was perfect for her needs. Moments later, I envisioned nails as a carpenter might have used in another age, and there before me was an old nail. Remembering festival debris in Chinatown, I came upon a cluster of ragged trees hung with faded streamers. Passing an inaccessible pile of red bricks, I wished for a chunk to write with, and around the corner such a chunk awaited, along with a small tablet-shaped stone that seemed to materialize just as I thought of it. The sky darkened, and as high winds swirled, I picked up my pace with a flush of excitement, my pockets brimming with treasure.

Later, braving torrential rain, I met with the congenial staff of the museum and was free to closely observe the work of Jan van Eyck and fine examples of his powerful influence on those yet to come. I stood before the panel of Gabriel, with wings the color of a sliced African fig, across from that of Mary, the folds of her robe swathed in light. I bowed my head and said a little prayer for my sister. It was February 16, her birthday, and I was reunited with the panel that inspired our clandestine adventure, over a decade ago, producing a slightly out-of-focus Polaroid that I shall always cherish.

And the pieces fell about me like snow, forming a picture of winter. A stretch of time when I was rewarded with so many mystic moments, a chunk of red chalk, a chestnut, a rusted piece of scrap metal, a nail, and a flat stone shaped like an ancient tablet. Although suggesting little of the magnificence of the work I had seen, these objects helped to inspire my newfound contentedness. I placed them with the same care as a police detective into a clean plastic bag. Evidence of an awareness of the relative value of insignificant things.

THE VANISHED GLOBAL ENTRANCE PANEL

ON THE PLANE I WATCHED *2001: A Space Odyssey*, drifting just as the ape reached out to touch the monolith. I slept through most of the flight and dreamed that the missing panel of *The Righteous Judges* floated to the surface of the Baltic Sea in a black body bag. "It is found!" cried a euphoric public. However, in a complex courtroom scene it was decreed it must remain zipped up, lest it crumble into the wanton dust of the future. There were ensuing arguments, but I was tapped on the shoulder just as conclusions were being drawn. I fastened my seat belt as the plane circled Newark Airport and wrote it all down on a wide napkin that I accidently tossed into a trash can when I cleaned out my pockets on the way to customs.

My brief journey served to remind me that there are universes within universes and a fluent society comprehending the value of small things, provided by fate to guide one in crossing paths littered with unforeseen obstacles. Standing in line, I received a message that my petition to obtain global entry had been denied as I am a resident of New York. Punitive measures pressed by the present administration upon a state that has at least some amount of compassion for those in need of sanctuary.

There must be good in the world

THE PANEL FOR THE
EMERALD OF JUDGMENT

IN A DESPERATE SEARCH FOR A VACCINE, no less than twenty-five hundred macaques were purposely infected with a deadly strain of coronavirus. These macaques were identified as laboratory monkeys, as if a species of their own, coming into being solely to be in service to humankind. Their sickly faces were not those of the bright, mischievous monkeys who reigned in the lunar year of 2016. Would a panel of lively rats actually be capable of cheering them up? One day we may be judged for their sacrifice, which can hardly be called consensual. I try to block the image of their sad eyes peering through wire cages as they wonder what will become of them, and us all for that matter.

The act of writing in real time in order to deflect, escape, or slow it down is obviously futile yet not entirely fruitless. Even as I write this epilogue to an epilogue, I am aware that it will be obsolete by the time you read it. Yet, as always, I am compelled to write, with or without true destination, lacing fact, fiction, and dream with fervent hopes, then returning home to sit at the desk that was my father's and transcribing what I have written.

Sam and I used to commiserate on being dogged by the incessant urge to write, whether it got anywhere or not. It strikes me how blessed I have been to have had him to talk to for the good part of my life. We were human buoys, sustaining each other's work, even through his most difficult struggle, one that he won spiritually but lost as a human on earth.

I am on my own now, but I guess I can still talk to Sam, just as I do with other beloved souls that don't seem dead at all. I can revisit the land of late-night conversation, when Sam would call from Kentucky and we'd talk about all kinds of things, from traveling on barges to navigating loneliness. We often pondered on why writers, in the pursuit of producing the unclassifiable, are generally coerced into attaching a label identifying a work as fiction or nonfiction. Both of us relished the prospect of writing a book so uniquely faceted that one would be hard-pressed to distinguish one from the other.

Before saying good-night, I'd implore him to tell me again the story of Cortés and the Emerald of Judgment, occasionally falling asleep, phone in hand, before he ended. The story begins with a gift from Montezuma to Hernán Cortés, a palm-size emerald the color of the sea, at least nine hundred carats, fastened to a leather strap. It was rectangular in shape like a tablet inscribed with the sacred words of law. And this emerald was said to have mystical properties, guiding Montezuma in his decision-making.

Sam's versions were ever-changing, somewhat removed from history, now fragmented in memory like shifting trailers of a film. I can project certain images of Sam's stories upon the opened panels of a massive triptych. The centerpiece depicting the ruthless explorer bobbing in the abyss, one arm vertically extended, the leather strap wrapped about his thick wrists, the emerald cutting into his clenched fist, the side panels brandishing the turbulent sea, the warring waves of Turner.

From the deck of the ship, Cortés is hurled into the maelstrom. Nature views him with amusement. The fellow has exceedingly little horse sense. Is he willing to die for it? He cannot eat or drink it, so why such a passionate effort to save it? The boiling sea spits him out, and he is saved, holding fast to his prize. Yet in the end nothing is truly gained. Cortés fails to grasp the gem's transcendent worth and is granted no more power than the Nazis in possessing the very spear rumored to have pierced the side of Christ. The spear was thought to have divine properties, but they drew nothing from it. For such objects possess their own code, notably that it is essential that the golden scales be tipped toward the good. For there must be good in the world in order that the world prevail. Petitioned with a charitable heart, even within its stoic silence, the Emerald of Judgment, as the oracle Montezuma believed it to be, would tell you that.

Jerry Garcia, Fillmore West

POSTSCRIPT PANEL

AT 4 A.M. I AM AWAKENED by the angry repetitive cries of a man somewhere in the streets below. From my window I can see the silhouette of the Peace Tower as clouds dragging across the bruised sky expose a bright smear of the full worm moon. A siren goes off, and yet I can still hear him, half-wolf, half-human howling. There is a news alert that the entire population of Italy is under quarantine, a country in lockdown. I envision coffeehouses with golden espresso machines, museums, theaters, and the winding streets empty by decree. I think of Milan, where gracing the wall in Santa Maria delle Grazie is Leonardo's *Last Supper*, its shimmering remains keeping a ghostly vigil over the frightened Latin provinces. Cloistered, they wait for the virus as if its a looming barbarian invasion. And here is where I leave us, with catastrophic strategy rivaling prudence. I close my journal in the dressing room at the Fillmore West, where it all began, on my sixty-ninth birthday, ushering in the Year of the Monkey. In the historic corridor I join the band, pausing before the alcove where the image of Jerry Garcia smiles upon us, mounting the stage with hopes that our jubilant play will provide a measure of collective joy.

New York, Ghent, San Francisco

ILLUSTRATIONS

Images on pages 76 and 124 are public domain.

All photographs © by Patti Smith

Patti Smith is a writer, performer, and visual artist. She gained recognition in the 1970s for her revolutionary merging of poetry and rock. She has released twelve albums, including *Horses*, which has been hailed as one of the top one hundred albums of all time by *Rolling Stone*.

Smith had her first exhibit of drawings at the Gotham Book Mart in 1973 and was represented by the Robert Miller Gallery for three decades. Her retrospective exhibitions include the Andy Warhol Museum, the Foundation Cartier, and the Wadsworth Atheneum Museum of Art. Her books include *Just Kids*, winner of the National Book Award in 2010, *Witt*, *Babel*, *Woolgathering*, *The Coral Sea*, *Auguries of Innocence*, *M Train*, and *Devotion*.

In 2005, the French Ministry of Culture awarded Smith the title of Commandeur des Arts et des Lettres, the highest honor given to an artist by the French Republic. She was inducted into the Rock and Roll Hall of Fame in 2007.

Smith married the musician Fred Sonic Smith in Detroit in 1980. They had a son, Jackson, and a daughter, Jesse. Smith resides in New York City.